THE
L. G. WRIGHT
GLASS COMPANY

James Measell

W. C. "Red" Roetteis

Dedicated to the memory of
Lawrence Gale "Si" Wright (1904-1969)
Verna Mae "Toots" Wright (1914-1990)

FOREWORD

In 1976, barely one year out of the service and very ignorant of the printing and publishing business, I was suddenly thrust out of my comfortable office chair and into the car as a traveling salesman for the family printing business. My territory was described to me as "running the river," which meant that I was to cover all the Ohio River Valley from Pittsburgh to Ashland, Kentucky.

If you are much of a glass enthusiast, you will immediately recognize that the area I just described encompasses dozens of towns that were homes to glass factories. Many were already clients of Richardson Printing, but others had never heard of the company I represented.

Over the years I successfully sold printing to twenty-five or more glass companies. I developed friendships with some of the principals of these factories and worked on hundreds of catalogs and sales sheets and helped them market their glass. But there was one factory where I never sold a thing — and never got past the showroom door. That was the L. G. Wright Glass Company in New Martinsville, West Virginia.

As a consequence, I became fascinated with the company and the glass they sold. I tried to learn all I could about Si and his wife and the glass, but in the 1970s, no one seemed to know very much about them.

As the years went by, the mysteries lingered. Did they actually make glass? Whose moulds were they using? Did some of their glass end up in antique stores? These and dozens of other questions went unanswered. And it looked like they never would be answered.

I have a philosophy about glass and glass collecting. I believe that if you hang around the glass business long enough, you'll cross your own path. And once again I've seen that statement prove true. For in the production of this book, I've finally gotten past the showroom door. Thanks to Phyllis Buettner and her mother Dorothy Stephan, Jim Measell and Red Roetteis were able to research and write the definitive story of Si Wright and his wife Verna Mae and the L. G. Wright Glass Company. And I was able to get those intriguing questions answered. I even discovered, much to my surprise, that my eclectic collection contains a few cranberry opalescent pieces once sold by L. G. Wright.

The story of the L. G. Wright Glass Company is a great story and one that's never been told before. One of the joys that comes with my job is the opportunity to see incredible collections of glass and to share those collections and what we learn about them with other people via the photographs and the information in our books. And we've done it once again with this book on L. G. Wright. My hope is that you will draw as much enjoyment from reading Si Wright's story and learning about his glassware as we have had presenting the story to you.

David Richardson
Publisher

For about six decades, the L. G. Wright Glass Company has conducted its business from the small town of New Martinsville, West Virginia. Yet, this firm has remained generally unknown to the American glass collecting public for many years. Its founder, L. G. "Si" Wright, was a private man, and the company did not advertise its wares or distribute a retail catalog. Nonetheless, some pioneer glass researchers, such as Minnie Watson Kamm and Arthur Peterson, learned of the Wright company and mentioned some of its glassware, but the extent of the Wright line was a well-kept secret. Churchill's words are appropriate: "...a riddle wrapped in a mystery inside an enigma."

Now, the story of the L. G. Wright Glass Company can be told. We have had complete access to the company's archives—from the first checkbook and the earliest customer invoices to the most recent catalog sheets and interviews with past and present employees. We have had the full cooperation of the present owners, Dorothy Stephan and Phyllis Stephan Buettner. We hope that the result of our research is a full and complete portrait of Si Wright and his glass company.

James Measell
W. C. "Red" Roetteis
August, 1997

ACKNOWLEDGEMENTS

This research project owes a great debt to the current proprietors of the L. G. Wright Glass Company, Dorothy Stephan and Phyllis Stephan Buettner. They helped in every possible way, from allowing freedom of access in company records to preparing glassware to be photographed (and even serving lunch to hungry guests!). They and other L. G. Wright employees were always enthusiastic about "our book," even when confronted with frustrations and delays.

This book was really the brainchild of former Wright salesman W. C. "Red" Roetteis, who has sold, bought and loved more L. G. Wright glass in the past three and one-half decades than most glass collectors ever knew existed! Red mentioned his idea for a book on L. G. Wright glass to Nancy Fenton, director of new product development at the Fenton Art Glass Company, when they met at a gift trade show out West. Nancy said that Red ought to "contact Dave Richardson and Jim Measell at Antique Publications," and Red soon followed through on her suggestion. I'm glad he did, for the opportunity to meet, talk and work with Red has been a rare privilege indeed.

Many people helped construct the biographies of Si and Verna Mae Wright and the history of their company. Early employee and salesman Gene Carr shared his memories and records to help me understand just how the company start-ed and developed. Ernie Loy and Gene Beegle provided remarkable details and insights about Wright's dealings with glass manufacturers, decorating firms, suppliers and distributors. Gloria "Ticky" Baniak and Rick Hoskins recalled the beginnings of the decorating department and offered anecdotes about the Wrights, too.

Photographers James and Paul Pappas were most cooperative in identifying their work for Wright. Frank M. Fenton allowed access to the records of the Fenton Art Glass Company's production of Wright glass, and he recalled various aspects of his business relationship with Si Wright between 1948 and 1969.

Many people loaned glassware or other items so that they could be included in this book. Others offered information via interviews or correspondence. My thanks go to them all: Michele Binetti, Sharon Bland, John Gentile, Lucile Kennedy, Willard Kolb, Carolyn Kriner, Kent Longwell, Charles Mason, Holly McCluskey, Curt and Carol Montmon, Debbie Moody, Christine Roberts, Harold Ruble, Patty Sue and George W. "Sonny" Sebar, Franklin Smith, Geraldine Stone, Delbert "Bud" Ward, and John and Tom Weishar.

Terry Richards Nutter created the layout and design of this book under extraordinarily pressing deadlines.

James Measell
August, 1997

Contents

MYTHS AND MISCONCEPTIONS

Because of all the intrigue surrounding the L. G. Wright Glass Company over the years, a number of myths and misconceptions—not to mention just plain misinformation—have been promulgated about L. G. Wright and his glassware products. These sorts of statements often take on lives of their own, and some persons will, no doubt, resist the dispelling of these myths and misconceptions despite all evidence to the contrary.

MYTH #1:
L. G. Wright was the very first to reproduce American pattern glass.

Advertisements for reproductions of the Horn of Plenty pattern appeared in *The Magazine ANTIQUES* before Wright graduated from high school, and the Phoenix Glass Company began to advertise some of its milk glass reproductions several years before Wright entered the glass business as a sales representative in the mid-1930s. The Wright firm began in 1937-38.

MYTH #2:
All L. G. Wright glass was made by the Fenton Art Glass Company in Williamstown, West Virginia.

Perhaps because the story of Wright's involvement with Fenton has been told so candidly (see *Fenton Glass: The Second Twenty-Five Years*, pp.9-10 and *Fenton Glass: The Third Twenty-Five Years*, pp. 59-60) and there has been so little written about Wright's relationships with other manufacturers, this myth has persisted. In fact, Wright's glass was made by many different American factories, including some of the industry leaders: Bailey; Dalzell-Viking; Davis-Lynch; Fenton; Fostoria, Gibson; Imperial; Morgantown; Mosser; New Martinsville; Paden City; Plum; Rodefer; Summit; Venetian; Westmoreland; Wilkerson; and Viking.

MYTH #3:
All L. G. Wright glass is "cheap" glass.

This myth carries the implication that Wright glass is of inferior quality. While Wright negotiated firmly to hold down his costs and sometimes bought "seconds," the wholesale prices of Wright's glass for his customers are comparable with those listed by other glass manufacturers for similar wares and comparable colors. Wright's customers ranged from small gift shops to large department stores and mail-order retail catalog houses, so poor quality could not be tolerated.

MYTH #4:
All L. G. Wright glass was made from original old moulds.

Although Wright's customers (and Wright himself) often liked to emphasize the idea of original moulds, the overwhelming majority of Wright's production actually came from new moulds—commissioned and paid for by the L. G. Wright Glass Co. The company's files contain hundreds of invoices for moulds produced by National Mould and Machine, Stiehm & Son, Island Mould and Machine, and Albert Botson's B. Machine & Mould.

This myth owes its strength to the vivid, but fanciful tales of moulds squirreled away in caves and rumors of thousands of old moulds hidden behind stout walls and locked doors. Wright did indeed purchase a cache of moulds from the old plant in Indiana, Pa., which had housed the Northwood and Dugan firms, but they were relatively few in number when compared to the volume of new moulds.

In her pioneer articles in the *American Collector* during the late 1930s and in the 1940s, Ruth Webb Lee noted the detail differences between Wright reproductions and old glass time and time again. These differences, of course, result from the use of new moulds which are unlike the originals. Furthermore, Lee also reported seeing Wright glass in department stores and gift shops.

MYTH #5:
L. G. Wright glass was made in large quantities.

Most of the time, Wright contracted for glass to be made in a given color in rather small quantities, typically a few hundred at a time. Items which sold well were made regularly to maintain inventory, but many articles remained in stock for months or even years before they needed to be produced again.

MYTH #6:
L. G. Wright glass had limited sales.

At first glance, this statement actually seems to contradict the myth above! Although Wright glass was far from even approaching the sales volumes of Cambridge, Fenton, Fostoria, Heisey, Imperial or Westmoreland, it can be argued that Wright's market niche--Victorian-style reproductions--was a significant one, especially since the "big" factories made some of these kinds of items, too.

Wright's sales representatives covered the entire United States, and Wright glass was displayed in several of the large merchandise marts in major cities. Because Wright glass was available only on the wholesale level for so many years, the consumer public was generally unaware of the Wright name.

MYTH #7:
L. G. Wright made "fake" antiques.

While there is no doubt that some of Wright's customers misrepresented the age of the glassware when they resold it, there is likewise no doubt that the L. G. Wright Glass Co. was simply a wholesale distributor of glass made from its own moulds. The long-term success of the business depended upon steady volume, not upon the quick sale of a few high-priced "fakes" prior to disappearing from the scene.

This myth stems from the near hysteria which began to develop in the 1930s when Ruth Webb Lee's articles began to appear in American Collector and her book *Antique Fakes & Reproductions* was first published. Dealer/author George S. McKearin had a display of "glass forgeries and reproductions" in his Hoosick Falls, New York, shop in mid-1937. Other writers later branded some splendid American pattern glass motifs as "pitfall patterns" simply because some articles in the line had been reproduced.

MYTH #8:
L. G. Wright reproduced everything in pattern glass.

Another outgrowth of the irrational reaction to reproductions, this myth also perpetuates the mystery surrounding Wright's activities. In fact, several American glass companies were selling reproductions in the 1930s and 1940s. Although many of these reproductions were discussed in Lee's articles for *American Collector* between 1938 and 1946, the manufacturers were never identified. Although Hammond's Confusing Collectibles pictures many L. G. Wright items, the company is not always named. By the 1960s and 1970s, many American glass factories were making reproductions, including those which were done especially for some of the nation's most prestigious museums.

GETTING STARTED IN GLASS, 1936-1939

Lawrence Gale Wright was born September 25, 1904, to Silas and Rosa Wright. His parents farmed and kept livestock on Terrapin Ridge outside of New Martinsville, West Virginia. Wright grew up knowing the hard life of a farm family, and, when he graduated from Magnolia High School in 1925, he was determined to make a different path for himself in the world.

His father was known as "Si" and Lawrence was sometimes called "Young Si," although he also became known simply as "Si" (correspondents incorrectly addressed him as "Cy" for years). Among Wright's memories was the scene of his father shaving on an outdoor porch before an oval, wood-framed mirror surrounded by beautiful roses growing around the supporting posts. Years later, this recollection would inspire the Mirror and Rose pattern. In a similar manner, the likeness of an farm outbuilding where Wright's first glassware was stored would become the Wright logo decades later.

During the early years of the Great Depression, Wright worked on the farm and delivered meat to shops in New Martinsville. One

Rosa and Silas Wright

family story holds that the destruction of a newly-harvested crop of strawberries in a barn fire convinced him that he ought not to trust Mother Nature to provide!

Wright found brief employment in the rubber industry in Akron, Ohio, but, by 1936, he was back in New Martinsville. He became a sales representative for the New Martinsville Glass Manufacturing Company. Factory invoices show that Wright often sold to A. A. Sales near St. Louis, a concern that later bought glassware from the L. G. Wright Glass Co.

Wright's travels in 1936-37 brought him into contact with glass and pottery manufacturers in the Ohio Valley, and he decided to make a living by buying glassware and pottery "seconds" and re-selling them to wholesale customers. He also sold some glass and pottery to the public at carnivals and fairs, but his real interest was in the wholesale trade.

Wright also had a business card which said simply "Antiques." He may have been a picker for some antique dealers, and he soon acquired knowledge of American pattern glass. Publication of Ruth Webb Lee's *Early American Pressed Glass* in the early 1930s stimulated interest in this field

L. G. WRIGHT
NEW MARTINSVILLE, WEST VA.

NEW MARTINSVILLE GLASS
MANUFACTURING CO.

L. G. WRIGHT
NEW MARTINSVILLE, WEST VA.

Antiques

THE L. G. WRIGHT GLASS CO.

New Martinsville, W. Va.

Represented by:
LAWRENCE WRIGHT

THE L. G. WRIGHT COMPANY

NEW MARTINSVILLE, W. VA.

Represented by
LAWRENCE WRIGHT

by naming patterns and standardizing terminology. Because of the scarcity of early blown glass. collectors were turning to nineteenth-century pressed wares with increasing enthusiasm. Price-guide booklets such as the Caurtman House "Comparative Values of Pressed Glass" began to appear. S. T. Millard's well-illustrated book *Goblets,* released in 1938, further focused the attention of glass collectors on major American-made pressed patterns.

Wright soon ascertained those patterns from the nineteenth century which were becoming popular collectibles—such as Bellflower, Daisy and Button, Baltimore Pear, Hobnail, Ivy in Snow, Rose in Snow, Three Face, Lion and Westward Ho. The Westmoreland plant had made Westward Ho goblets in 1936, and Wright was surely aware of their reception in the marketplace.

In *Fenton Glass: The Second Twenty-Five Years*, a story is recounted wherein Si Wright had Fenton make a Hobnail barber bottle for him in the 1930s. This article may have appeared at a New York glass trade show. The first Wright inventory (1938) lists barber bottles in amber and vaseline glass. The Wright barber bottle also inspired the Allen B. Wrisley Company of Chicago to contract with Fenton for the design and production of a similar Hobnail perfume bottle which is fitted with a wooden stopper.

Wright's earliest business was a cash operation, and he likely kept no books, simply living from transaction to transaction. In the summer of 1937, however, he opened a checking account at the First National Bank in New Martinsville when his company was about to be born. There was some indecision about its exact name, and business cards for both the L. G. Wright Company and the L. G. Wright Glass Company were printed.

On August 2, 1937, Si Wright used his first checks to make glassware purchases from the

Fenton Art Glass Co. and the Cambridge Glass Co. He soon bought glassware from the Morgantown Glass Co. and the Westmoreland Glass Co. All of Wright's customers for 1937 are not known, but he did a good bit of business with A. A. Sales.

Late in 1937, he contracted with the National Mold and Machine Works of Clarksburg, West Virginia, for the manufacture of a plate mould, the first of four plate moulds made during 1937-38: Rose and Snow; Baltimore Pear; Daisy and Button; and Lion. Wright also had six other moulds made: Three Face goblet, Three Face wine, Three Face sauce, Lion goblet, Panel Grape goblet, and Baltimore Pear goblet.

These new moulds mark the real beginning of Wright's reproductions of popular American pattern glass items. Most came from the National Mold and Machine Works, while a few were made by the Stiehm & Son Mould and Machine Works, a Donora, Pa., firm. A $100 check to the Fenton Art Glass Co. (November 27, 1937) carries the notation "mold," but lacks any description (this could be the Hobnail barber bottle). Wright may also have done some business with the Overmeyer Mould Co. at Zanesville, Ohio.

Records from 1938, the first "official" year of the L. G. Wright Glass Co., offer a comprehensive picture of the firm's products. An early September letter (see next page) to Mrs. L. P. Fletcher of Painted Post, New York, lists the items available in the Wright line. All appear in the yearly inventory, along with a few other articles.

In 1938, Wright purchased about $5300 worth of glass from various manufacturers, about 60% from the New Martinsville Glass Co. Some $1500 came from the Fenton Art Glass Company, and the rest was divided among various firms. Among the items in Wright's 1938 inventory are these articles, linked to their places of manufacture: Kitten slippers (Fenton); Turkeys (Cambridge Glass Co.); Kitten and Rabbit plates (Westmoreland); and vari-

9

THE L. G. WRIGHT COMPANY

MANUFACTURERS
OF
PRESSED AND BLOWN GLASSWARE

NEW MARTINSVILLE, W. VA.

September 1, 1938

Mrs. L.P. Fletcher
Painted Post, N.Y. R #1

Dear Madam:

Received an order from you for several pieces of merchandise about which we thought it best to write you, listing the items, colors, and prices and in that way we will not make any mistakes in shipping you merchandise.

We would like for you to look this list over and make up a new order and send it to us.

Westward Ho Goblets	$ 9.00 doz
" " Sauces	9.00 doz
Daisy and Button Goblets Asst. Colors	7.20 doz
" " " Sq. Plates Blue,Vaseline, Amber, Crystal	6.00 doz
Moon and Star Goblets	9.00 doz
Pineapple "	9.00 doz
Rose and Snow " Asst. Colors	7.20 doz
Baltimore Pear "	12.00 doz
" " Plates	1.25 ea.
Three Face Sauce Dishes	2.00 ea.
Rose and Snow Plates Asst. Colors	1.00 ea.
Barber Bottles Amber, Vaseline	5.00 pr.
" " Cranberry Red,Opalescent Blue	4.00 ea.
Hobnail Cream Pitchers Cranberry Red and Opalescent Blue	4.00 ea.
" Cruits Cranberry Red and Opalescent Blue	4.00 ea.
Candy Stripe Swirl Water Pitchers	3.00 ea.
Blue Opalescent Sq. Mouth Dotted Water Pitcher	3.00 ea.
Duck Salts, Milk, Green	3.00 doz.

Will have several new items by the 20th of Sept.

We wish that you would make your order from the above list and send it to us at once.

Very truly yours,

L.G. Wright Co.

LW:VW

THE L. G. WRIGHT COMPANY

MANUFACTURERS

OF

PRESSED AND BLOWN GLASSWARE

NEW MARTINSVILLE, W. VA.

" 1938 Inventory "

7	dozen - #2 Basket ----------------	@ --	$ 3.00 -	$	21.00
6	" -- #3 " ----------------	@ -----	4.20	----	25.20
48	" ----- D. and B. Goblets --------	@ -----	1.50	----	72.00
28	" ----- " " " Plates, round -	@ -----	3.50	---	98.00
29	" ----- " " " " square-	@ -----	1.35	----	39.15
35	" ----- Rose and Snow " --------	@ -----	1.35	----	47.25
42	" ----- " " " Goblets ---	@ -----	1.50	-----	61.00
6	" ----- Westward Ho " ------	@ -----	2.25	----	13.50
4	" ----- " " Sauces ---	@ -----	2.75	----	11.00
5	" ----- Moon and Star Goblets --	@ -----	1.50	----	7.50
1	" ----- " " " Bowl -----	@ -----	6.00	----	6.00
6	" ----- D. and B. Pannel Goblet Blue, Amber --------	@ -----	3.50	----	21.00
14	" ----- Horn of Plenty Tumbler --	@ -----	2.00	----	28.00
18	" ----- Pear Goblets -----------	@ -----	1.50	----	27.00
1-1/2	" ----- Grape " -----------	@ -----	1.50	----	2.25
7	" ----- Thumbprint Goblets, R.S.-	@ -----	3.94	----	13.58
12	" ----- " Crystal ----	@ -----	1.02	----	12.24
1	" ----- Hand Vase -------------	@ -----	4.50	----	4.50
5	" ----- Fan Trays ------------	@ -----	3.00	----	15.00
7	" ----- Kitten Slippers -------	@ -----	1.80	----	12.60
1	" ----- Spot Pitchers ---------	@ -----12.00	----	12.00
20	only ----- Turkeys ---------------	@ -----	1.00	----	20.00
26	" ----- Barber Bottles, Cranberry	@ -----	1.50	----	39.00
14	" ----- " " Blue ----	@ -----	1.00	----	14.00
30	" ----- " " Am. Vas.-	@ -----	1.00	----	30.00
60	" ----- Hobnail Pitcher, Cranberry	@ -----	1.50	----	90.00
30	" ----- " " Blue ----	@ -----	1.00	----	30.00
20	" ----- " Cruits " --------	@ -----	1.00	----	20.00
18	" ----- " Vases " --------	@ -----	.75	----	13.50
12	dozen ----- Lion Goblets, Cry. Frosted	@ -----	2.75	----	33.00
3	" ----- " Plates ---------	@ -----	4.50	----	13.50
6	" ----- Three Face Goblet --------	@ -----	2.75	----	16.50
15	" ----- " " Wine -------	@ -----	2.75	----	41.25
4	" ----- " " Sauce -------	@ -----	3.00	----	12.00
1	" ----- Pear Plates -----------	@ -----	3.00	----	3.00
4	dozen - #1 Chicken, White --------	@ --	$ 3.00 -	$	12.00
2	" -- #2 " Black --------	@ ----	6.00	----	12.00
10	" -- #1 Duck White --------	@ ----	1.50	----	15.00
2	" -- #1 Camels " ---------	@ ----	4.20	----	8.40
5	" ----- Kitten Plates & Rabbit --	@ ----	3.00	----	15.00
1	" ----- Zodiac " Large --------	@ ----	6.00	----	6.00
2	" ----- " " Small --------	@ ---	3.00	----	6.00
4	" ----- Turtles --------------	@ ----	4.32	----	17.28
3	" ----- Elephants ------------	@ ----	2.70	----	8.10
3	" ----- Bears ---------------	@ ----	3.24	----	9.72
2	" ----- Frogs ---------------	@ ----	2.70	----	5.40
190	" --#1 Slipper---------------	@ ----	.60	----114.00
79	" -- #2 " ---------------	@ ----	.76	----	60.04
138	" --#1 Hat ----------------	@ ----	1.00	----138.00
33	" -- #2 " ----------------	@ ----	2.00	----	66.00
12	" -- #3 " ----------------	@ ----	3.00	----	36.00

Total Stock on Hand $ 1451.46

ous covered animal dishes (Erskine Glass Co.). Other popular sellers were goblets, clarets and wines in the Kings Crown pattern, which was originally called X. L. C. R. ("Excelsior"). Wright placed many orders for Kings Crown from the Indiana Glass Company at Dunkirk, Indiana, and he also used these stemware moulds on a rental basis.

The largest quantities in Wright's 1938 inventory were two novelty items—slippers and hats. The slippers came in two sizes (designated #1 and #2), and the hats came in three sizes; all display a Daisy and Button motif. These hats and slippers were purchased from the New Martinsville Glass Co., and, in 1940, Wright arranged to buy these moulds. In 1938-39, E. and F. Jung of Buffalo, New York, were buying Wright's slippers and hats by the gross, and they quickly became a staple, remaining in the Wright line throughout the company's history.

Wright's sales for 1938 were $8,664.25, and his net profit was about $2500. He spent $1000 to acquire a frame building in the Brooklyn area on South Main Street in New Martinsville and owed another $1000 on the mortgage note. This building, a former harness shop, was home to the L. G. Wright Glass Company from 1938 to 1946.

In January, 1938, Si Wright attended the annual glass and china show at the William Penn Hotel in Pittsburgh. This wholesale exhibition brought him into contact with glass manufacturers, and it also enabled him to meet many independent manufacturer's representatives. These men maintained showrooms in major cities and took wholesale orders for glassware to be shipped directly from the company to the customer. The representatives typically had glassware samples from several different firms on display, and they were paid monthly commissions on their sales.

Two independent representatives—Frederick Skelton of New York City and Earnest Dower of Newburyport, Massachusetts—soon began to handle Wright glass for buyers in the East. Dower was particularly successful in selling assortments of the slippers and hats to customers from New England who visited his showroom in Boston's Parker House hotel. In a letter to Dower (September 10, 1938), Wright said he was "very well pleased with the orders that you are sending in" and expressed the hope that "this business will amount to something this coming fall."

The earliest typewritten customer invoices in the Wright archives are from February, 1938. At this time, the company letterhead described the firm as a manufacturer and wholesale dealer of "art in glass, china and brass." A few months later, a revised letterhead reflected a sharper focus, namely, "manufacturers of pressed and blown glassware."

The early invoices afford a remarkable look into the glassware items and colors marketed as L. G. Wright glass. In March, 1938, for example, notes on invoices mention Wright's new line of Hobnail barber bottles in amber, cranberry and vaseline [these were made by Fenton]. In writing to one customer, Wright said "we are sure these will be good retailers." Individual orders seldom totalled more than twenty dollars, but Mrs. Don Hoover (Quincy, Illinois), Henry Rassler (Louisville, Kentucky) and the Virgin Mercantile Store (Omaha, Nebraska) bought large amounts of Wright glass.

During 1938, Wright traveled extensively by car throughout Western Pennsylvania, Ohio, West Virginia, Virginia, Tennessee, Kentucky, Indiana, Illinois, Iowa, Missouri, and Kansas. Today, stories abound concerning Si Wright

---

THE L. G. WRIGHT COMPANY

MANUFACTURERS
OF

PRESSED AND BLOWN GLASSWARE

NEW MARTINSVILLE, W. VA.

January 17, 1939

This letterhead was used for many years.

hawking glassware from the back of a station wagon, and these accounts have the ring of truth. Wright called upon gift shops and department stores, but many of his most important customers were antique dealers who maintained individual shops in towns or along major highways.

Wright subscribed to the Lightner Publishing Company's *Hobbies* magazine, one of the few periodicals which carried antique dealers' advertisements describing antique glassware for sale. Many of the dealers whose names appear regularly in *Hobbies* during the late 1930s and early 1940s became Wright's customers, and quite a few of them purchased glass from him for years thereafter.

There is no doubt that some who bought Wright glass later misrepresented it as "old" and sold it as such. During World War II, a few dealers sold this glassware though the mail and deceived their customers. Others, operating under the principle of *caveat emptor*, simply priced the glassware reasonably and put it in their shops, mixed in among the old pieces.

Those who operated combination antiques and gift shops recognized the sales potential of glassware which reflected old motifs but carried a much lower price and was available in wholesale quantities. When one antique dealer inquired about Three Face sauce dishes and Lion goblets, Wright replied simply: "we are cheaper than anyone else making reproductions."

Today's glass collectors, ever alert to re-issues and reproductions (domestic and imported), may find it hard to imagine a time when there were few books devoted to antique glass and little worry among customers about the age or authenticity of items found in antique shops. Ruth Webb Lee's *Early American Pressed Glass*, published in the early 1930s, made no mention of reproductions. Demand for collectible old glass fueled a market for low-priced, new glass which was inspired by the old patterns and motifs.

Victorian-style epergnes had been made in the 1920s and advertised to dealers in *The Magazine ANTIQUES,* along with imitation cut glass, china and porcelain. Reproductions of pressed glass—such as Bellflower, Horn of Plenty and Westward Ho—began to appear in the retail gift shop and department store market. L. G. Wright understood this demand phenomenon, and he capitalized upon it, building his business during the late 1930s by having moulds made and working hard to expand his sales.

On May 16, 1938, L. G. Wright married Verna Mae Haught. He called her "Toots," and this affectionate term became well known to the company's employees and wholesale customers. The couple had no children, and the L. G. Wright Glass Company soon became their life together. Si took charge of sales and negotiations for getting the glass made, and Toots kept the books meticulously and typed the invoices and correspondence. Over the years, the demands of their business were such that they rarely took vacations, although they often travelled together to glass shows in New York or Pittsburgh.

In May, 1939, L. G. Wright purchased a number of moulds as well as a polishing lathe and glassmaking tools for $600 from John R. Richards, an Indiana, Pa., businessman who had been associated with several glass companies. These moulds included patterns and novelties associated with the Northwood Glass Company and its successors, the Dugan Glass Company and the Diamond Glass-Ware Company. The Diamond firm had been destroyed by fire in June, 1931, and it was not rebuilt due to disagreements among the stockholders and the hard financial times.

Shortly after the fire, executives from the Fenton Art Glass Company had journeyed to Indiana and purchased a few moulds and some fixtures which were removed to Williamstown, West Virginia. It might seem surprising that the rest of the moulds remained in Indiana for nearly eight years, but one must remember that these were old patterns and items whose popularity had long since waned. Given the economic climate of the 1930s, the glass factories which were just getting by could ill afford to risk capital by buying the moulds. Si Wright saw opportunity, however, and he seized it, writing a $100 check on May 5, 1939, as a down payment on the moulds. Soon thereafter, he borrowed $500 from the Union National Bank in Sistersville, pledging a herd of beef cattle for collateral.

Some of the moulds were in working order, and Wright's investment soon began to pay off. The 1939 L. G. Wright year-end inventory lists the Corn vase and the Dolphin compote as well as the Pump and Trough. These remained in the Wright line for many years, although the available colors changed from time to time. Moulds

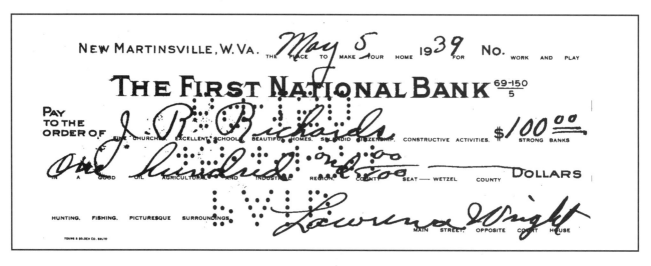

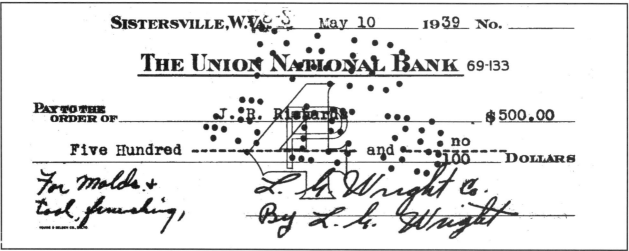

Checks for the Indiana, Pa., moulds.

for the Cherry pattern were in this acquisition as were the Daisy and Fern spot moulds for blown opalescent ware. This latter motif was a fixture in the line for decades, and pitchers, tumblers and cruets are mentioned in the 1939 records.

Wright purchased about $3500 worth of glass in 1939, more than half from the Fenton Art Glass Company. These items were mostly blown ware, and they ranged from Hobnail barber bottles in various colors to cranberry pitchers with crystal handles. Wright also had several new moulds made during 1939. Stiehm & Son completed the Lion egg cup mould about May 1, and other invoices refer to a "fancy" goblet and plate. The 1939 Wright inventory lists goblets and plates in Daisy and Button, likely the "fancy" pattern.

A new Fenton product in 1939 was "Peach Blow," a cased glass which is opal (opaque white) with an inner layer of pink. Peach Blow bowls and vases quickly became features of the

Wright line. Beginning with its Blue Ridge, Fenton was also beginning to develop "crest" lines, and this treatment would become important to the L. G. Wright Glass Co. in the 1940s.

Wright also continued to buy some glassware for resale from various glass plants. Purchases came from the New Martinsville Glass Company (slippers and hats) and the Indiana Glass Company (Kings Crown stemware and Lords Supper bread plates). The 1939 inventory also lists Candlewick plates (from Imperial) and Cambridge Glass Co. covered Turkeys as well as many items in Ivy in Snow and a few in Blackberry.

The two latter patterns, which originated before the turn of the century, had been revived by the Phoenix Glass Company of Monaca, Pa., in the late 1930s. Wright visited the Phoenix plant in early 1939, talking with president Thomas W. McCreary and arranging to sell the Phoenix's

INDIANA GLASS COMPANY

MANUFACTURERS
OF
PRESSED AND BLOWN GLASSWARE

DUNKIRK. IND.. U. S. A.

DATE SHIPPED

SHIPPING DATE

SOLD BY
mail

CUSTOMER ORDER DATE

SOLD TO   Lᵍ.Wright Co.

New Martinsville, W.Va.

CUSTOMER ORDER NO.

TERMS   SHIPPED TO   ROUTE SHIPPED

This bill is subject to 1 per cent discount if paid on or before
Feb. 20   , after which date positively
NO DISCOUNT WILL BE ALLOWED.   30 DAYS NET.
LL GOODS SOLD F. O. B. DUNKIRK. IND. NO ALLOWANCE FOR BREAKAGE.   CLAIMS FOR OVERCHARGES MUST BE MADE IMMEDIATELY ON RECEIPT OF GOODS.

PACKAGES	DOZ.	DESCRIPTION	PRICE	AMOUNT	TOTAL
1 bbl	8	Lord's Supper plates cry. (1.00)	3.48	27.84	
1 bx	1	Lords Supper plates colored figures bronze back cold color (.33)	7.20	7.20	
				35.04	
		less 50%		17.52	
				17.52	
					17.52
1 bx	6	77 wines 3 fire ruby	5.10	30.60	
2 bx	6	77 goblets 3 fire ruby	6.92	41.52	
				72.12	
		less 40%		28.85	
					43.27
					60179
		1 bbl/1.00 1 bx./.33			1.33
					62.12

Invoice from the Indiana Glass Company; the "77" goblets and wines are the popular King's Crown pattern.

lines of antique-style glassware (Blackberry, Ivy in Snow and Lace Dewdrop) when he called on his customers. Phoenix made Ivy in Snow and Blackberry in both milk glass and crystal, and Wright's 1939 inventory lists numerous items. Ruth Webb Lee (*American Collector*, April and September, 1941) discussed these Blackberry goblets and reported they were being sold in a Texas department store for $12.50 per dozen.

The first several years are the most difficult for any new venture, and L. G. and Verna Mae Wright could surely have testified to this statement. By dividing the tasks but working together, they established the L. G. Wright Glass Company and were striving to increase its business. The next decade, witnessing a world during war and its aftermath, would bring new challenges.

THE 1940s: GROWTH AND EXPANSION

In general, the war years were positive ones for American glass firms. There was some loss of skilled glassworkers who were in the Armed Forces, but imported glass from the European continent came to a standstill. Wright continued to buy some glass for resale from various firms, especially the Fostoria Glass Company at nearby Moundsville, but it seems clear that he was moving strongly to establish a line of Early American-style glassware made with moulds he controlled.

During World War II, some American importing firms—such as A. A. Sales, Koscherak Brothers Inc., and F. Pavel—turned to domestic suppliers for utilitarian and decorative glassware. Wright sold glass to A. A. Sales in the late 1930s, when this firm wanted the slippers and hats. In 1940-41, A. A. Sales was buying these and other glass novelty items from Wright. The A. A. Sales' letterhead said "wholesale to dealers" and mentioned "antiques, pattern glass [and] novelties" (incidentally, this concern later became known as A. A. Importing and still markets reproductions of antiques today).

The Koscherak firm was particularly interested in Wright's table centerpiece epergnes. These large, showy items consisted of a heavy base with upraised center, glass and metal fittings, and four trumpet-shaped vases (or "cones" as they are sometimes called)—a large one at the center and three identical smaller ones arranged symmetrically. These moulds were made by Joseph Weishar's Island Mould and Machine Co. During WWII, Fenton produced the bases and trumpet-shaped vases (often in opalescent glass or with various crest treatments) while the nearby Paden City Glass Manufacturing Company pressed the glass fittings in crystal. Wright brought these components to his warehouse in New Martinsville, added metal fittings (purchased from E. H. Schwab, a Pittsburgh firm), and packed the final product in a large carton for shipment .

Wilmer C. "Bill" Fenton, who was then attending Marietta College and working summers at the Fenton Art Glass Company, recalls that Fenton "made those epergnes by the hundreds for L. G. Wright to sell to the Koscherak Brothers during the war." In Fenton's archives, a notebook compiled by salesman Robert C. Fenton, Jr., records about twenty items being priced to L. G. Wright. Cream pitchers, milk pitchers, "jugs" [water pitchers] and finger bowls are listed; these were likely in cranberry glass as well as blue opalescent. The "Corn Cob" vase is mentioned as are the Pump and Trough and the Dolphin compote.

The Koscherak firm was instrumental in the development of L. G. Wright's Panel Grape and Moon and Star pattern lines. A Koscherak brochure from the mid-1940s lists nineteen different Panel Grape items; most were available in opalescent blue or crystal, and the crystal could be had with "Natural Color Decoration ... ruby grapes

Wright epergne (made by Fenton)
in Koscherak brochure, c. mid-1940s.

WHOLESALE TO DEALERS

ANTIQUES   -   PATTERN GLASS   -   NOVELTIES   -   STAMPS

A. A. SALES CO. Inc.

6508 DELMAR BLVD.
UNIVERSITY CITY, MO.

Jan. 29, 1940.   193___

PHONE CAbany 0270

L. G. Wright Co.,
New Martinsville, W. Va.

Dear Mr. Wright:

   Due to the illness and death of the writers
Mother we have been unable to take care of our correspondence
until now.

   On going over your invoice we find everything O. K.
with the exception of the one charge for the 6 only handled mugs
which you had listed at 50¢ instead of 35¢ as previously purchased
from you and are remitting as follows:

```
                Invoice amounting to            $55.95
Less overcharge on handled mugs as stated above    .90
                                                 55.05
                            Less 1%                .55
                            By Check             54.50
```

   We would appreciate hearing from you as to how
the moulds for the two plates you were making are getting along
and to the approximate time you expect to have these ready.

   Hoping you are enjoying a good business, we are,

      Yours very truly,

      A. A. SALES CO. Inc.

P. S. We are herewith enclosing "Shippers Form and would kindly
 ask you to complete same for the shipment stated above.

and green leaves." Wright employee Ernie Loy recalls taking crystal Panel Grape articles to a decorator named Myers in Washington, Pa., who, in turn, shipped the finished glassware to Koscherak.

The Koscherak brochure also depicts a Daisy and Fern pitcher and four pieces of Moon and Star. The pitcher, a shape seldom seen today, was available in either cranberry or opalescent blue. The Moon and Star items were available in crystal or opalescent blue, and these items are shown: 9"

Price List PANEL GRAPE Line
in Transparent Crystal

Prices are NET, for repacked and carton quantities.

Items illustrated	Open Stock Dz.	Min. Dz.	Cartons Dz.	Min. Dz.
62/65C Covd. Sugar (or Candy Jar)	$14.40	½	13.20	1½
62/67C Pint Cream	9.00	½	8.25	1½
62/61C Water Tblr. 9 oz.	5.40	1	5.00	4
62/60C Ftd. Parfait	6.50	1	6.00	4
62/63C Celery Vase	9.75	½	8.75	1
62/57C Bowl 8"	10.50	½	9.75	2
62/58C Nappy 5"	6.00	1	5.50	2½
62/59C Fruit 4"	5.00	1	4.50	6

Prices and details of full stemware line in crystal listed on page 3, shapes as illustrated on page 2.

•

Also available in Natural Color Decoration on crystal (ruby grapes and green leaves), shapes as shown on page 2

	Open Stock Dz.	Min. Dz.	Cartons Dz.	Min. Dz.
56/49 Goblet	$10.80	1	$10.00	4
56/48 Sherbet	10.80	1	10.00	4
56/47 Cocktail	10.20	1	9.75	4
56/46 Wine	10.20	1	9.75	4
56/45 Cordial	9.60	1	8.75	4
56/44 Ice Tea 14 oz.	10.80	1	10.00	4

PANEL GRAPE items shown above are carried in transparent Crystal only. In addition, all the articles shown in Opalescent Blue on preceding page are obtainable in crystal.

Panel Grape items in Koscherak brochure (c. mid-1940s); note the mention of "natural color decoration."

footed salver; 8" open compote [called "footed bowl"]; 6" covered candy box; and 10" high footed covered compote.

The war effort led to rationing of materials and gasoline, and L. G. Wright found himself unable to travel, making it impossible to call on accounts personally, let alone attempt to open new areas. He approached a newcomer to the New Martinsville area, A. C. [Audrey] Roetteis, who was driving regularly throughout Western Pennsylvania, Ohio and West Virginia in his job for a manufacturer of wooden barrels. Roetteis's company was involved with some war work, so he had ration cards to purchase gasoline.

For several years, they travelled together as Roetteis called on various mills and Wright sought customers for glassware. Typically, Wright was dropped off in town with a box or two of samples, and Roetteis would pick him up several hours later. The men shared a liking for thoroughbred racehorses, and Roetteis later built Paducah Farms on the outskirts of New Martinsville.

In 1941, the L. G. Wright Company had about $8900 worth of glass made; over $7200 came from the Fenton Art Glass Company, and more than $1100 from the Paden City Glass Manufacturing Company. Gross sales were nearly $16,000 (almost double the volume for 1940), and the company invested more than $1200 in new moulds to expand the line.

In 1940 or 1941, Wright began to work with Joseph Weishar's Island Mould and Machine Company in Wheeling (this enterprise, headed by grandsons Tom and John Weishar, remains in

Price List PANEL GRAPE Line
in Opalescent Blue

Prices are NET, for repacked and carton quantities.

		Open Stock Dz.	Min. Dz.	Cartons Dz.	Min. Dz.
*62/29B	Goblet	$ 8.50	1	$ 8.00	4
62/45B	Sherbet	8.50	1	8.00	4
62/46B	Cocktail	8.25	1	7.80	4
62/47B	Wine	7.80	1	7.50	4
62/48B	Cordial	7.50	1	7.20	4
62/49B	Ice Tea 14 oz.	8.50	1	8.00	4
62/50B	Salad Plate 6½"	8.25	1	7.80	4
62/56B	Plate 10"	12.75	1	12.00	3
62/62B	Ind. Cream	8.40	½	7.80	4
62/68B	Ind. Open Sugar	8.40	½	7.80	4
62/64B	Covd. Jelly Comp.	15.60	½	14.50	1½

*Goblet also available in solid white Milk Glass.
62/29W at same price as Opalescent Blue.

Price list of the same items in transparent crystal:

		Open Stock Dz.	Min. Dz.	Cartons Dz.	Min. Dz.
62/8	Goblet	$ 6.50	1	$ 6.00	4
62/45C	Sherbet	6.50	1	6.00	4
62/46C	Cocktail	6.00	1	5.50	4
62/47C	Wine	5.25	1	4.80	4
62/48C	Cordial	5.00	1	4.50	4
62/49C	Ice Tea 14 oz.	6.00	1	5.50	4
62/50C	Salad Plate 6½"	6.00	1	5.50	4
62/56C	Plate 10"	10.20	1	9.50	3
62/62C	Ind. Cream	7.50	½	6.95	4
62/68C	Ind. Open Sugar	7.50	½	6.95	4
62/64C	Covd. Jelly Comp.	12.00	½	11.40	1½

The FAMOUS PANEL GRAPE design, now offered for the first time in a full range of Stemware, Tumblers, Plates and Accessory Table Articles.

Pieces illustrated are the Opalescent Blue. Also available in Transparent Crystal. See page 3 for further details and prices.

Panel Grape items in Koscherak brochure (c. mid-1940s).

business and is widely recognized as an industry leader). The Island firm crafted many new moulds during the 1940s for Wright, and these helped the company grow.

Joe Weishar was a highly-skilled mouldmaker, and his shop had a strong reputation for its ability to turn out a top notch mould in short order to meet a customer's needs. Invoices from 1941 show that Weishar made the large Atterbury-style Duck and matching base moulds for Wright as well as moulds for a custard cup, a rose bowl, and a finger bowl. One intriguing entry on an invoice dated October 24, 1941, reads as follows: "cutting figure deeper in antique nappy." This probably refers to repair work done on one of the moulds purchased earlier in Indiana, Pa. By 1944-45, Island Mould had also produced quite a few

Panel Grape and Moon and Star moulds for Wright along with moulds for lamp parts.

On December 24, 1945, L. G. Wright made an advance payment of $4000 to Weishar as part of an agreement for "moulds to be shipped when completed, over a period of two years." John Weishar chuckled when he saw this old agreement, and he recalled his grandfather's stories regarding Wright's frequent attempts to barter with a combination of cash, freshly-butchered hogs and bushels of corn and potatoes. "Grandpap was wise to get the cash up front," John said. "Si really loved to bargain."

Shortly after the end of World War II, the L. G. Wright Glass Company took several giant strides forward. The first was the construction of a new building south of New Martinsville, just off West

December 24, 1945.

Received of Lawrence G. Wright, Four Thousand
Dollars ($4,000.00) as payment for glass moulds to be
manufactured by the Island Mould & Machine Company; the
above Four Thousand Dollars ($4,000.00) being paid in
advance and the moulds to be shipped when completed, over
a period of two (2) years.

ISLAND MOULD AND MACHINE COMPANY

By *J. D. Weishar*

Joe Weishar and Si Wright maintained a close business relationship throughout the 1940s, and their respective firms grew and prospered.

Monthly Statement

Wheeling, W. Va., *May 2* 1941

The L. G. Wright Co
New Martinsville
W va

In Account With

Island Mould and Machinery Co.

78 MARYLAND STREET

Phone 1533

1941					
Mar	14	Balance	32	00	
	15	Custard Cup	25	00	
	21	Duck Pug.	4	00	
	21	Formers	34	79	
Apr	4	Finger bowl,	35	00	
	4	Pug,	35	00	
	30	Goblet Figure	28	00	
			2	193	79

"MOON & STAR" reproduction in Salvers, Bowls, Candy Boxes and Comports in Opalescent Blue, also available in transparent Crystal. "Fern" design Jugs in opalescent optic Cranberry and Blue.

Four Moon and Star pieces and a Fern pitcher from a Koscherak brochure (c. mid-1940s).

Virginia State Route 2 . The structure was a plain concrete block edifice encompassing offices, a sample room, and plenty of storage space for the glassware inventory in an intricate series of well-built wooden bins. Wright had an antenna installed on the roof, and his friends often gathered on Sunday evenings to enjoy one of the first television sets in the New Martinsville area.

A. C. Roetteis recalls Wright talking about his "dream" in the early 1940s when the two men travelled together. Wright envisioned a complex of buildings which included warehouses, mould storage, a decorating shop, offices and an adjacent home. When Roetteis built his Paducah Farms in 1945-46, Wright borrowed the architectural plans.

The first building served the Wright firm well for about a decade before it was expanded. Later, additional units were built, along with a comfortable ranch-style home. Acting as his own contractor, Si Wright supervised the design of these structures closely, and the L. G. Wright Glass Company's buildings reflect the knowledge he gained from observing the decorating, packing and shipping operations in the many glass factories he had visited.

The area around the L. G. Wright plant and home was beautifully landscaped, and many evergreen trees and shrubs were planted, along with a multitude of colorful flowers. Wright was a longtime subscriber to the *American Nurseryman* publication, and he sometimes spoke of plans for a Christmas tree farm and other similar ventures.

In 1947, Verna Mae's cousin Gene Carr—who had been employed by Wright as a packer since January, 1946, and helped construct the first building—decided to visit some armed service buddies in Florida. Carr talked to Si about taking glassware samples and attempting to write orders along the way. He recalls having cranberry pitchers and tumblers plus other pieces to show, and this endeavor proved to be quite a success.

Carr persuaded Si to let him go on the road to sell Wright glass. For about three years, Carr traveled throughout the United States, opening numerous new accounts for Wright glass. While working the Great Lakes region in 1947, he inaugurated an important relationship between the Wright firm and the Carl Forslund enterprise of Grand Rapids, Michigan. Later, Carr was particularly active in the Southeast and Southwest.

In the mid-1950s, after other salesmen had been added, Carr's territory was everything west of the Mississippi River, and there were rules to follow. Carr was not to contact existing accounts, and he was not to solicit new business within 50 miles or so of established accounts. Despite these strictures (and having to pay his own expenses), Carr continued to seek new prospects for Wright glass, calling upon large stores and small shops as well as some antique dealers.

Upon arrival in a town, Carr would peruse city directories and the telephone "Yellow Pages" for department stores and gift shops. "I always tried to sell the 'better' stores," he said in an interview in 1996, as he displayed two thick ledger books detailing the many accounts he opened over about a nine-year period.

Si Wright (second from left) and friends at the 1938 Kentucky Derby.

The names of Carr's accounts reflect a time in America when there were few department store chains, and cities typically had one or more family-owned stores offering a wide variety of merchandise, including glassware: Cain Sloan (Nashville); C. J. Gayer (Mobile); Mass Brothers (Tampa); The Boston Store (Ft. Smith); Denver Dry Goods; A. Harris and Son (Dallas); Zion Cooperative Mercantile Association (Salt Lake City); The Marston Store (San Diego); Buffum's (Long Beach); Wilshire House Wholesale (Beverly Hills); J. W. Robinson (Los Angeles); City of Paris (San Francisco); Frederick and Nelson (Seattle); Spokane Dry Goods; and the Hellgate Trading Post (Missoula)

Carr read avidly about glass in books and magazines devoted to antiques, and he convinced Wright to use the phrase "Early American" in describing the company's glassware. Customers remembered Gene Carr for his soft-spoken personal style, and he often suggested that they display Wright glass in window settings reminiscent of the many picturesque antique shops along major thoroughfares.

It took Carr several years to break even financially, but his efforts opened Texas, California, and the entire Southwestern U. S. to Wright glass. High shipping costs were then a problem for dealers in the West, so Carr frequently reduced his commissions to secure an initial order and get the customer started with Wright glass. Later, he sold in the Great Lakes area, before this territory went to Don Jennings. Parts of the East Coast were covered by Si Wright's cousin Elzie Yoss, who lived in Wheeling.

Gene Carr recalled the difficulty of selling glassware by showing samples. "It took quite a while to set up the ware for a presentation," he said, "and I spent a lot of time unpacking and packing." He suggested to Wright that good color photos of the glassware in the line would be effective sales tools.

As it happened, photographers James and Paul Pappas had set up a new business in

This original photo shows Wright products from the 1940s. The Dolphin compote (upper left) and the Trough and Pump (upper right) were made from original Northwood moulds.

Parkersburg after they left the service following WWII. The brothers were seeking photography work of all kinds, and Jim went up and down the Ohio Valley calling upon various concerns—including glass and pottery companies—to talk to them about using high quality dye-transfer color photos to show their merchandise. These were relatively expensive photos, but color printing was not yet perfected, and the photos were great improvements over black-and-white shots.

"I was practically living out of my car," Jim Pappas remembers. "I called on Si Wright, and he

Wright's first new building, under construction in 1946.

contracted with us for color prints to be used by his salesmen. Paul and I did the first photos in late 1947 in the sample room upstairs at the plant in New Martinsville." Crystal items, such as Three Face and Westward Ho, were shot in black-and-white on a dark background.

The finished color prints had cloth hinges attached and were arranged in binders. A typewritten price list was prepared to go in accompanying small notebooks, and each salesman got a set of color photos in a binder along with a price list notebook. The lists were updated as items were discontinued and prices revised, but the color photos remained unchanged for some years due to the expense of re-shooting the glassware.

In the fall of 1948, the Wright firm introduced several new products which were destined for success—the Moon and Star toy lamp (crystal, blue, amber and milk glass), the amber Turtle, and the 7" covered Hen on Nest in a new color,

"amberina." Both the Moon and Star lamp and the Turtle remained in the line for many years, and the Hen on Nest generated great interest in the new color.

The amberina effect is achieved by pressing items in a selenium-based ruby glass. The glass emerges from the mould as amber or straw-colored, and then selective warming-in achieves the rich ruby highlights. Glassmakers sometimes call the amberina effect "ruby half-struck." Within a year or so, the Cherry cream and sugar were offered in amberina along with the Dolphin compote and Daisy and Cube goblets and wines.

At the close of the 1940s, Wright glass was becoming increasingly popular. The cost value of the company's inventory grew from $25,800 in early 1947 to $37,500 at the end of 1949. The next twenty years would bring considerable expansion and growth, further establishing the L. G. Wright Glass Company name across the nation.

BOOM TIMES: THE 1950s AND 1960s

This twenty year period marks great growth and success for the L. G. Wright Glass Company. Glassware was its main interest, and Wright began a glass decorating department in early 1968. At about the same time, a ceramics department was added. In 1969-1970, the organization had, for the first time, total sales of more than $1 million.

Wright glassware was becoming known nationwide through an increasing number of sales representatives, several of whom maintained showrooms and exhibited at major giftware shows in the United States. Wright glass appeared in retail mail order catalogs, including those of the prestigious Carl Forslund furniture manufactory in Grand Rapids, Michigan.

Many new moulds were made by B. Machine & Mould, a Cambridge, Ohio, establishment operated by mouldmaker Albert A. Botson. This shop was very good at chipping the pattern in a mould, but some factories experienced difficulties with the hinges or had other production problems. Nonetheless, there are invoices or other records for more than four hundred Botson-made moulds in the Wright files.

Botson's relationship with Wright began in the mid-1950s, and he made about two dozen new moulds during the first year. Botson's invoices to Wright, which also included repairs and alterations to old moulds, totaled over $6000 for 1956. In 1960, Botson's work amounted to over $10,000.

About 1953, Wright began a business arrangement with glassmaker Salvatore "Sam" Diana, who operated the Venetian Glass Corporation in Rochester, Pa. Little is known of this small enterprise. Glassmaker John Gentile, son of glassmaker Peter Gentile, recalls his father's association with Sam Diana, including Diana's visits to the Gentile home in Morgantown, West Virginia, and long sessions of "briscola," an Italian card game played with great enthusiasm.

Diana may have been associated with the Beaver Valley Glass Co. near the close of World War II, shortly before starting his own operation in rented quarters within the William A. Meier Glass Co. A fire almost put Venetian Glass out of business in March, 1948. At the time, the magazine *Retailing* listed its products as "wine, whiskey and beer glasses and novelty glassware items."

Wright contracted for glass with Diana, and he also bought some items from the Venetian's line for resale. The latter consisted of goblets, wines

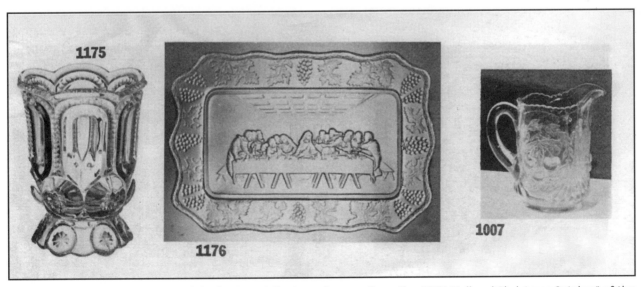

Three pieces of glass from the Wright line are at the top of a page from the 1953 "Fall and Christmas Catalog" of the Vermont Crossroads store in Waterbury, Vermont. The store said the Moon and Star spoonholder was "made from the original mold" and the Cherry creamer was described as "not antique although it certainly looks it." The Lords Supper bread plate was purchased by Wright from the Indiana Glass Co. in Dunkirk.

VENETIAN GLASS CORPORATION
DIANA HANDCRAFT — GIFT LINE
LAMP PARTS
AMERICA'S FINEST HAND BLOWN AND HAND MADE GLASS
371 CLEVELAND STREET
ROCHESTER, PA.
PHONE: SPruce 4-4960

and sherbets which have a thin blown cranberry bowl and a crystal stem and foot; these were in the Wright line about 1959-60.

The Venetian Glass Corp. made blown lamp parts (such as cranberry glass shades) and other glassware for Wright from 1955 through about 1963. Some was heat-sensitive "Peach Blow" (pink inside, opal outside), a color typically associated with Fenton's production for Wright. Nonetheless, the Venetian made rose bowls, barber bottles, covered candy boxes, salt shakers and several styles of vases, including the "picture" vase. These were also made by Venetian with opal inside and pink outside.

Some of the Peach Blow ware (particularly the picture vases) made for Wright by either Fenton or the Venetian firm was decorated by another Rochester firm, the Zarilla Art Glass Co. Operated by Pete Zarilla, this small concern also decorated Wright lamp parts and some of the large "wedding" bowls. Inspired by some decorated china, Wright developed a Moss Rose decoration which was quite popular.

During the 1950s and 1960s, Wright glass was often shown in catalogs issued by Carl Forslund, Inc., a Grand Rapids, Michigan, furniture manufacturer who produced splendid booklets filled with excellent color photos of furniture in room settings and lots of "folksy" copy. The Forslund firm took pride in quality and great customer service, as this excerpt from the 1954 catalog reveals: "We're open every day except Sunday, and even then, just give us a call, one of us will be happy to take you through our place."

Glass appears often as accents in the Forslund furniture groupings, and the catalogs offer many different Wright articles for sale. In the Forslund catalog for 1959, Wright glass occupied six pages, including three in full color. Forslund dubbed the glassware "Owl Hollow" glass, and lauded the pieces as "replicas of early American pressed glass Victorian novelties," often implying that old moulds were used. The namesake for the phrase Owl Hollow is an area  between Sistersville and Paden City, West Virginia.

The 1961 Forslund Christmas catalog mentions L. G. Wright with this effusive (but not entirely accurate!) praise: "Mr. Wright of New Martinsville, West Virginia, has made for many, many years, all of our replicas of American Early Glass and we have become close friends too—besides our business association. He is a perfectionist and probably the most learned scholar of blown, pressed antique glass along the Ohio River Valley, although such a modest gentleman. Mr. Wright takes justifiable pride in his exacting

ZARILLA ART GLASS CO.
DECORATORS OF
QUALITY GLASSWARE
800 VIRGINIA AVENUE EXT.
ROCHESTER, PA.

Your Order No.

Sales Office No.

SOLD TO

Our Order No.

9-6
L.G. Wright Glass
New Martinsville, W. Va.

Via   picked up by Bi

Shipped to

Net 10-6

F. O. B. FACTORY
SUBJECT TO USUAL PACKAGE
CHARGES

TERMS: 30 Days Net or 1% Discount 15 Days from Date of Invoice   Overdue Accounts Subject to Cash in Advance.

PKGS.	DOZS.	DESCRIPTION	PER DOZ.	EXT.	TOTAL
	69 pcs. (1 br).	large 1523-13" bowls asstd decors	1.75		120.75

Hand Blown Barber Bottle

with Genuine West Indies
"Kissin' Sweet" Bay Rum

The smell of Bay Rum on a man is a good smell . . . a medley of sunlight and good morning kisses and crisp apples and polished leather all translated into a single fragrance to splash on a freshly shaven face. We've secured tall bottles of Bay Rum distilled in St. Thomas by a family who has been in the business since pirate days! With it comes an old-fashioned barber bottle of hand-blown glass in cranberry and opal. Makes a swell gift for your favorite male! Complete set, tax included......... **$5.95**

P.S. This copy was written and given to us to use by a nice New York City customer who ordered one of our wine-sized replacement bottles of Bay Rum—$2.00 postpaid and tax paid—her husband has used our Bay Rum since their honeymoon!

Wright's cranberry opalescent barber bottles were packaged with Bay Rum aftershave lotion in this interesting ad in a mail order catalog.

reproductions, he personally watches each one as it is blown or pressed, and so many are broken by his order as they do not meet his exacting standards of good replicas."

The 1962 Forslund Christmas catalog furthers the mystique, calling Wright a "rather shy man" and relating that he "collected discarded old iron and steel moulds of original glass patterns when he was an apprentice glass-blower." The 1966 Forslund catalog adds even more picturesque flavor in discussing decorated Wright pieces—referring to an "artist grandma" from Owl Hollow itself and an "elderly, shy artist [from] Martins Ferry."

In the early 1960s, Si Wright contracted with the Pappas brothers for a new series of dye transfer color prints. These were integrated into spiral binders with heavy, clear plastic sheet protectors. A mimeographed price list, prepared painstakingly by Verna Mae, faced each photograph. These spiral binders were used by the sales force until the first L. G. Wright Glass Company "Master Catalog" was photographed by James and Paul Pappas and printed at their Park Press in 1968.

Wright glass price lists were issued yearly between 1961 and 1967, and these served to keep the salesmen informed of new articles as well as price changes and items withdrawn from the line. The 1963 Wright glass price list was devoted to "exclusive gifts in Early American glass and colonial lamps of yesteryear," and the front cover said simply, "Early American Glass Is Our Hobby."

Between 1950 and 1970, most of the Wright line (except for lamps) was pressed ware. Blown ware—such as cranberry, cranberry opalescent and blue opalescent or decorated vases in milk glass—remained popular, but there were few instances of overlay colors such as Peach Blow, except for items in the new Maize pattern in the mid-1960s. The emphasis seems to have been on pressed glass in a variety of standard colors.

Although some articles (such as individual goblets, Westward Ho and Three Face) were made only in crystal, the following colors were in the line continuously from 1950 to 1970: amber, amberina, amethyst, blue, green, pink, ruby and vaseline. The amberina color had been introduced in the late 1940s, and the number of items grew steadily in the 1950s. The c. 1962 salesmen's binders featured several entire pages devoted to this interesting color. Ruby and amberina were slightly more expensive than the other pressed ware colors.

Dark blue and dark blue satin were also produced (especially in animal covered dishes), along with some "slag" (purple slag), also for animal dishes. Post-war restrictions on uranium made vaseline glass a bit harder to come by, but both Fenton and Viking made it for Wright from time to time. The epergnes with distinctive crest *text continued on page 33.*

The next several pages show Wright glassware depicted in Carl Forslund catalogs.

Sunshine Catchers

OWL HOLLOW REPLICAS OF EARLY AMERICAN PRESSED GLASS VICTORIAN NOVELTIES

Our men can pack a large order about as fast as a small one, so we can offer you a saving. If your order for glass pieces is $20.00 or more, deduct 10% of the total. Fair enough?

CITY GASLIGHT LAMP

Cranberry glass with opalescent polka dots and 8¼″ fluted shade. Both chimney top and round font are electrified. Milk glass Gothic base. The lamp is 24″ tall. Price, including prepaid express.............. **$39.95**

ABOVE *Top Row* EXCITING GIFTS

No. 241—Did you know the Owl Hollow colors were as lovely as this? The round Moon-and-Star Bowl is 11″ across. In blue only. Postpaid (all pieces are) $7.75

No. 242—The Apothecary Jar, in rich cranberry only, is 10″ high. It's $15.25 . . . or a pair for your mantel........$29.95

No. 272—Beaded Grape Covered Compote, shown in amber; also in milk glass, amethyst or blue. Each $4.10

Here's our (non-electric) Daisy-and-Cube Oil Lamp, 9″ high, in the amberina color, $9.95. Or choose blue, amber, green or milk glass at.....................................$7.95

ABOVE *Bottom Row* CONVERSATION PIECES

No. 243—The pretty Lemonade Pitcher is clear sunshine yellow with opal "ruffle." Holds 3 pints, costs $11.00. Its companion No. 244 Tumbler is frosty sunshine-satin color, $3.35. A set? The Pitcher and six Tumblers, all for $29.95

No. 245—The beaded "open melon" footed Ivy Bowl is hand blown in opalescent sunshine yellow. A nice gift.......$2.35

No. 246—Footed Conch Shell Bowl, for dining table centerpiece or your mantel, in hard-to-find amberina $8.90

RIGHT *Top Row* RARITIES IN PATTERN GLASS

No. 92—The Corn Vase, 7″ tall, is a design brought to Pennsylvania from England. Choose this sunshine yellow or blue..$3.10

No. 2—Paneled Daisy-and-Button Goblet, in ruby as shown, $3.10 or six for $17.90; amberina, same price.

No. 223—Stippled Star Goblet, shown in amber (3rd in row) and blue (6th in row); also in green and amethyst at $2.20 each and $12.60 for six. Available in ruby red and milk glass, too, at $3.10 each and six for...........................$17.90

No. 1—Strawberry-and-Currant Goblet, 6½″ tall, is shown in green, $2.20 each, six for $12.60; also in amethyst, blue and amber at the same price. In ruby or milk glass, $3.10 each and six for $17.90

No. 2—The sunshine yellow Daisy-and-Button Goblet is the same pattern as the ruby goblet to its left, but a different price: $2.20 each and six for $12.60. Also in amethyst, blue, green and amber at this price.

No. 247—The Toothpick Holder (for every table) is Daisy-and-Button pattern, sunshine yellow color. Price $1.50

No. 3—Paneled Grape Goblets are shown next to each other in ruby red and amber. In ruby (or milk glass), the price is $3.10 each, $17.90 for six. In amber (or blue, green or amethyst), $2.20 each, for six $12.60

No. 248—Here again is the Lemonade Tumbler, this time in clear sunshine yellow like the Pitcher; $3.35, six for $19.10

No. 249—At the end of the row is the Daisy-and-Cube Goblet in ruby red, $3.10 each, six for $17.90; milk glass and amberina, same price; blue, green and amber, $2.20 each, six for $12.60

BELOW *Middle Row* SOMETHING FOR EVERYONE

No. 250—High-flying Compote, with beaded open pedestal, shown in sunshine yellow; in green and amber, too $2.40

No. 251—Graceful Goblet in ruby red (or amberina), $3.10 each and $17.90 for six. In blue, green or amber, $2.20; six . $12.60

No. 252—Moon-and-Star Wine Glass (folks grow ivy in 'em), in sunshine yellow as shown or amber, blue, green or amethyst, $1.75 and six for $10.25. Also ruby or amberina, $2.20 and six for $12.90

No. 253—Swirled cranberry and opal Cold Milk or Lemonade Pitcher, a beautiful ornament and always handy $8.80

No. 254—Ruby Horn of Plenty Goblet, $3.10 each, six for . $17.90

No. 255—Barber Bottle in ribbed sunshine yellow only (but what could be a happier color?) $6.00

No. 256—Ruby red Compote in Strawberry-and-Currant pattern . . . . : $3.10

No. 257—Round Cruet (furnished with a ground glass stopper) is Fern pattern in our sunshine-satin color. A bright idea . $6.65

BELOW *Bottom Row* "NEW" IDEAS FOR GIVING

No. 258—Daisy-and-Button Covered Compote, 4″ square, in sunshine yellow (hiding behind the kitten) $3.35

No. 245—Beaded Ivy Bowl, shown in blue and also stocked in amber, green and amethyst $2.20

No. 259—Daisy-and-Button Sugar and Creamer, in amberina color, complete set $6.20

No. 260—Covered Wicker Basket, in amber glass $1.65

No. 261—Cranberry Swirl Pitcher, lovely in sunlight $8.80

No. 262—Daisy-and-Button Four Wheel Cart . . . an ashtray, or for cigarettes . . . blue, amber, amethyst and green $2.20

No. 263—Buttermilk Swirl Goblet, a bit higher in price, but the prettiest of them all, we think . . . in ruby, $3.35 each, $18.65 for six. Or in blue, green or amber, $2.75 each, for six . . $15.35

The Kitten Sitting Up says, "Your friends will love these gifts of glass . . . or send ME . . . for just $9.95."

Christmas Shines so Softly...

My, wouldn't it be nice if we could afford to have our front stoop spilling over with pretty things like a big Candy Bag? We'd all like that. Possibly, it's the family love inside this door at Blake's that really counts—the others are just props and go back into stock after the photograph is taken. But they are awfully pretty and if some Oil King wants the whole porch full— we'll "blow the whistle"—the lot $339.20, and individually . . .

A By the light of this handsome Peter Marsh English Lantern-imported exclusively by us— your house says "Welcome" so cheerfully, doesn't it? 15″ high and projects 10″ from the wall. Prepaid $39.95

B Vicky Lee Lamp in soft blue color, 18″ high. Prepaid $25.20

C The American Beauty Lamp. Frosted white with a peach blow interior, that glows a soft pink color. 20″ tall, shade 11″ wide and the base lights, too. Prepaid $44.85

D Abby Lee Lamp with moon and star design shown in the most popular Amber color, but also stocked in blue or crystal, 20″ tall. Prepaid $24.95

E Dora Lee Lamp in Cranberry Satin glass with fern decoration. Lights in the base, too. Prepaid $39.85

F Bridget Lee Washstand—an authentic copy from the pre-plumbing days. 32″ high, 27½″ wide and 15¾″ deep. Available in both Dark Cherry or Buckwheat Honey finish. Prepaid $42.50

G Beth Lee Canterbury Magazine Stand — made with 23 hand turnings. 19¼″ high x 17¼″ x 14½″. In Dark Cherry or Buckwheat Honey. Prepaid $39.95

H Millie Lee — with lights in the base, too. Frosted amber, 19″ high. Prepaid $25.20

I Little Sue—a pert oil lamp in frosted blue, 8″ high. Postpaid $10.50

J Little Judy — embossed rose oil lamp, 9¾″ high. Postpaid $14.75

K Donna Lee — so many colors of rose come forth when this lamp is lit. 18″ high. Postpaid $31.50

REPLICAS OF VICTORIAN ODDITIES

No. 70 PUSS 'N BOOTS
in Daisy-and-Button pattern
GLASS SLIPPER

Just windowsill size, 6½″ long and 3″ high . . . in suncatching green, blue, amethyst and amber; milk glass, too. They're $1.65 each and $3.20 a pair. But why not buy one in each of the five colors . . . so nice to have ready for gifts or party prizes? Specially priced and sent postpaid, all five for $7.95.

No. 80 FAN-SHAPED GLASS BON-BON TRAY

The fan is an authentic replica in Daisy-and-Button design, with a raised edge that makes it a nice fancy dessert of birthday cake plate. Choose amber, blue or amethyst. Postpaid, $3.10 each; set of eight for dessert and coffee, express prepaid..................$24.00

No. 267 DAISY-AND BUTTON THREE PART RELISH DISH

Fill it with teatime tidbits and watch your visitors smile! It's 10¾″x4½″ and 3″ high, and we stock it in five sunshine colors, amberina, amethyst, blue, green and amber. Postpaid.. $2.95

No. 82 SUGAR SHAKER

We like to keep this full of sugar and cinnamon, so we can shake some on our butter-drenched toast and let it melt right in. But some folks keep one on the windowsill to catch the rainbows, and lots of people have one beside the bathtub, always filled with bath salts! The glass is rich cranberry red with milk glass swirls, 4½″ high. The price, postpaid, is.. $6.10

No. 92 BLUE CORN VASE

Sometime fill this 7″ Victorian novelty vase with celery and put it *on your supper table* . . . to start interesting table talk. (Also in sunshine yellow, page 57.) Postpaid..................... $2.90

No. 93 DAISY-AND-BUTTON KING SIZE ASHTRAY

Don't know what folks did with their tobacco ashes in 1890, as we've never found an old ashtray . . . Have you? But this is what we think they might have used, if everyone smoked then as they do today. Six inches square, in all the sunshine catcher colors—amber, amethyst, apple green and blue; or in sparkling clear crystal. Each $1.70

No. 108 THUMB-PRINT CRUET
Copied from a 6¾″ original made in the 1880's, complete with fluted handle. Choice of amber (sometimes called honey-gold, and shown in color on page 72) or emerald green. Postpaid, $6.45.

No. 109 TWINKLING STAR CRUET
A lovely replica with opalescent blue eye-dot design . . . like hundreds of twinkling stars in blue moonlight. See it in color on page 72 and buy it for $6.45.

No. 110 FAMOUS "DANCING S" CRUET
It's 8½″ tall and always available in peacock blue (page 72), amber (page 99), emerald green and milk glass at $6.45 postpaid. Also made in ruby red (hard to get) at $7.90.

Sunshine Catchers

FLOATING SWAN SALT DIPS

Bachelor son Jon, of all people, found an old original in soft, faded pink glass, and we got the glass blower who owns the old moulds to copy the same lovely geranium-pink color . . . knowing how lovely it would look on the table (with pink Vista china especially), possibly one by each plate, filled with nuts or mints, or loaded with sweetheart roses for a shower. In all colors . . . geranium-pink, old blue, amethyst, green, amber and milk glass. Each, postpaid, $1.10 . . . pair, $2.10 . . . six in assorted colors (or any single color you choose), $5.55 . . . dozen, $11.30.

treatments (made by Fenton) went out of the line in the 1950s. In the late 1960s, Wright introduced a large assortment of opaque Custard glass (some of which was decorated) along with Blue Milk Glass.

Of course, not every pattern or item was made in every color. The individual goblets and many novelties were typically in stock in amber, amethyst, blue and green, as were most patterns. Panel Grape was particularly popular in ruby, and both Daisy and Button and Moon and Star were good sellers in pink.

For some time, Wright had been marketing decorated glassware, particularly milk glass lamps. These were decorated at various places, ranging from the small Zarilla operation to the Bailey Glass Co., but the major supplier was the Davis-Lynch Glass Co. in Star City. Since Davis-Lynch had a decorating department, Wright could have glass made and decorated at the same location rather than sending an employee to pick up glass from a manufacturer, truck it to a decorating shop, and return later to pick up the finished ware to be taken to New Martinsville.

Among the decorators at Davis-Lynch was Gloria "Ticky" Mitchell (the precise origin of the nickname coined by her mother is now lost, even to Ticky herself!). She had been there since 1952, working in the lamp area of the decorating department. Her teacher and mentor at Davis-Lynch was Helen Rogers, who did the decoration designing. Ticky painted several Wright decorations on lamps, and she soon came to know Si Wright from his frequent visits to the Davis-Lynch plant.

Longtime employee Ernie Loy confers with a Lydon Bros. representative about the new decorating kiln.

Somehow, the idea of doing decorating for Wright in New Martinsville came up when Si and Ticky were talking. Wright liked the notion, but he was understandably concerned that the Davis-Lynch people (upon whom he depended heavily for glass lamp parts) might be unhappy if Ticky quit work. He discussed this with the owners, and there were no hard feelings when she left Davis-Lynch in early 1968. Davis-Lynch continued to supply the Wright firm with milk glass lamp parts.

Ticky and her sister June Mitchell (now June McCune) started work at the Wright plant in New Martinsville on February 14, 1968. June was in the shipping department, and Ticky, as supervisor of the new decorating department, was responsible for hiring and training the first decorators. They were Rick Hoskins, Freda Hubbard, Ruth Richmond, Alice Stout and Peggy Young.

In May, 1968, Gloria married John Baniak. He had worked at the Star City Bottle Company, but

Si Wright poses before the company display in a merchandise mart.

he came to be in charge of Wright's new ceramics department. Peg Woods of Clarksburg, West Virginia, was then helping Wright start a new giftware line. The production of Wright's distinctive ceramic Christmas trees began, and these proved to be both popular and long-lived, remaining in the company's catalogs for years. Another ceramic giftware line consisted of heavy gold leaf picture frames.

During many weekends in 1968-69, the Baniaks and June Mitchell traveled with Si Wright to glass and pottery shows in Ohio, Pennsylvania and West Virginia. They were always looking for ideas for new products or decorating motifs. As it turned out, Wright's sudden death in August, 1969, cut short a multitude of plans. As Ticky noted in 1996, Si Wright "had many dreams and so little time."

After Wright's death, Gloria and John Baniak stayed with the company for several years as Verna Mae Wright sought to maintain the business. In 1972, Gloria became head decorator at the Bailey Glass Co. in Morgantown, and John was foreman of the decorating department there. In 1974, they moved on to the Sinclair Glass Company in Hartford City, Indiana. Later, they went to McMinnville, Tennessee, where Gloria

was the sole decorator at B. & P. Lamp Supply Co. She retired in July, 1994, after working at B. & P. for about 18 years.

Gloria Baniak has fond memories of Si Wright, calling him "the kindest man I ever met." She recalls his dislike for school as a youngster because some classmates teased him with taunts of "Si Baby" and said he was a "dumb farmer." Later, when Wright was a successful businessman, he would look at some product and say aloud to himself, "Look what this dumb little farm boy has made!"

Although he was one of the first decorators, Rick Hoskins had actually worked at the Wright firm while in high school, and he came on full time after graduation in 1966. A young man blessed with artistic talent, his first project was the adaptation of Wright's Daisy and Fern motif for lamp parts. After studying an original Northwood mould from Wright's 1939 purchase, Rick pencilled the motif onto the whitened interior of a new spot mould so that Albert Botson could chip the final design. Both men had to work in reverse, of course, and they also had to plan for the expansion of the glass when it was blown into the final shape mould.

Later, Hoskins designed the 14" Bird vase

which was made in amber overlay (99-27), pink overlay plain or satin (99-28) and milk glass plain or satin (99-29). He recalls that Wright had him work from an antique vase with a leaf design, but Wright told him to "put some birds among the leaves." Some Phoenix Glass Co. products resemble this vase, so one of them may have provided the inspiration.

Hoskins also worked on Wright's Mirror and Rose pattern, developing the pickle jar and the salt/pepper shakers. After Si Wright's death, Rick Hoskins continued his education at the Cleveland Institute of Art, and he now works in the advertising field in Cleveland.

Although most of Wright's first printed catalog supplement was devoted to decorated lamps, some significant glassware made its debut. The Mirror and Rose pickle jar and salt/pepper shakers were shown, as was a line of more than a dozen pieces in pale blue opaque glass, including several animal dishes with milk glass heads.

In the mid-1960s, Kasmark and Marshall began to supply Tiffany-style leaded glass shades to the L. G. Wright Glass Co. Doing business as Kasmark and Marshall of Luzerne, Pa., these men had specialized in stained glass church windows (see next page).

The first Wright Master Catalog, c. 1968, shows table lamps with 12" d. "miniature standard" shades as well as large table lamps (shades 18-20" d.) and hanging shades (18-26" d.). The catalog had this to say about the shades: "The glass used in reproducing these shades is the same as used in the original shades. They require endless

hours of patient cutting and fitting to produce the inherent beauty of the old. They are made by very skilled artists who take pride in reproducing what we think are the most authentic shades to be had in this almost lost art."

Kasmark and Marshall worked closely with Wright to develop a series of motifs for the various shades. Rick Hoskins worked on many of these designs, and the large hanging shades and table lamps proved to be excellent additions to the Wright line, as customers were interested in antique reproductions. Records in the Wright files suggest that the glass was purchased from the Kokomo Opalescent Glass Co. in Indiana and from the Paul Wissmach Glass Co. in nearby Paden City.

The first page of Wright's 1969 Supplement displayed more than 30 pieces in "custard" glass, a hue popularized in America by Harry Northwood (who called it Ivory) and others in the 1890s. Wright's initial offering included about 20 pieces which were new to the line; several of these replicated old Northwood or Dugan patterns—such as Argonaut, Beaded Shell, Holly, Peacock or Twig—but most were made with new moulds. A few items were colorfully hand-painted by Wright's decorating department, and other decorated custard was made over the next several years.

Some custard pieces offered by Wright have a mark which closely resembles the underlined capital N in a circle trade-mark used at Harry Northwood's Wheeling plant for about a decade beginning in late 1905. Sharp-eyed collectors

Aerial view of the L.G. Wright Glass Company.

Four examples of the many Tiffany-style shades crafted by Kasmark and Marshall for L.G. Wright.

L. G. Wright glass is well-displayed at this gift show.

have noticed that this mark on some Wright pieces is not quite like the old Northwood mark because the upper left of the N nearly touches the circle. On other Wright pieces, however, the mark is quite difficult, if not impossible, to distinguish from the authentic Northwood trade-mark.

When the Fenton Art Glass Company was making some custard tumblers for Wright in 1969, company president Frank M. Fenton happened to see them as they came off the lehr and noticed the facsimile mark. "I thought it wrong to mark the glass in this way," he recalled, "and I told Mr. Wright that we would not continue to make these articles for his firm."

Subsequently, most of the Wright moulds bearing this mark were altered by adding a short line angled upwards from the lower left corner of the N. Some collectors now refer to this mark as "the wobbly W". In today's

flea markets and antique/collectible malls, one sometimes sees Wright custard items on which the altered mark has been ground in an attempt to restore the Northwood facsimile look. Incidentally, a glass collectors club, the American Carnival Glass Association, successfully brought suit against several individuals (not L. G. Wright) who had been involved with other glassware bearing a facsimile Northwood mark.

In 1969, a Canadian firm called Burke and Wallace Ltd. prepared a color flyer which illustrated some Wright glassware. Various "wedding" bowls were depicted, along with pickle castors in Daisy and Button, Mirror and Rose, and cranberry glass—all in elaborate plated frames and complete with tongs.

The strong sales and company growth of the 1950s and 1960s were cut short by the death of L. G. Wright on Friday, August 22, 1969. Employee Kent Longwell recalls that Si had complained of indigestion and some vague chest pain for a day

BURKE & WALLACE LIMITED

234 BELFIELD ROAD
REXDALE (TORONTO) ONT.

Presents Colonial Reproductions

Bride's Basket

1. **# 117 9" Milk Glass**
Mint Overlay
Hand Painted Yellow Roses

2. **# 117 9" Milk Glass**
Hand Painted Blue Roses

3. **# 117 9" Milk Glass**
Blue Overlay
Hand Painted Toy Roses

Pickle Cruets

A. **# 104 3 pc. Cruet**
w/Amber Mirror & Rose Glass

B. **# 104 3 pc. Cruet**
w/Thumbprint Cranberry Glass

C. **# 104 3 pc. Cruet**
w/Green Mirror & Rose Glass

D. **# 104 3 pc. Cruet**
w/Ruby Mirror & Rose Glass

E. **# 103 3 pc. Cruet**
w/Blue Daisy Button Glass

F. **# 103 3 pc. Cruet**
w/Amber Daisy Button Glass

G. **# 104 3 pc. Cruet**
w/Cobalt Daisy Button Glass

H. **# 104 3 pc. Cruet**
w/Amberina Daisy Button Glass

or two but shrugged it off and did not see a doctor. Rick Hoskins saw Wright stop to catch his breath while climbing the hill to the decorating department in the afternoon, and Gloria Baniak remembers that he looked pale and tired when he came in that Friday to fire the decorating kiln, a job he entrusted only to himself.

As usual, Wright had been working long hours. He was often busy late at night with Charlie Moore, a Pittsburgh Plate Glass chemist who was experimenting with heating glass in a modified glory hole and iridizing it with a spray to make a sort of "Carnival" glass. The fumes from this procedure were irritating and the procedure was laborious, but Wright hoped to make and market this glass successfully, and the nightly trials continued.

Early in the evening, Wright was outdoors and happened to gaze toward the nearby Wayside Furniture store. In the failing daylight, flickering reflections from an automobile's red tail lights in the store's windows made it appear that there was a fire. Wright jumped down from a retaining wall at the plant and quickly ran to the Wayside store. As it turned out, there was no fire, but the sudden exertion and excitement had taken their toll.

Later, Wright felt ill and decided to lie down on a couch at home to rest before dinner. After the meal, he returned to the couch, and Verna Mae later saw him apparently sleeping peacefully and did not try to awaken him. When she looked in again after the 11 p. m. news broadcast, she realized that he had passed away.

Funeral services for L. G. Wright were held on August 25, 1969, at Iams' Funeral Home in New Martinsville, the Rev. Ronald Casto officiating. Family friends A. C. and Cornelia Roetteis helped Verna Mae plan the funeral. Wright's pallbearers—Orgil Buck, Don Jennings, James Mayes, Charles Moore, George Setzer, and Elzie Yoss—were all associated with the glass company he had founded. Wright was buried in Northview Cemetery, although the gravesite was relocated later when Mrs. Wright arranged for a tall monument bearing a grape motif.

The *Wetzel Democrat* eulogized Wright as "founder and owner of the L. G. Wright Glass Co.," noting further that the company's "famed authentic antique glass reproductions are sold throughout the nation in many of the larger department stores." In Carl Forslund's 1970 catalog, Wright was remembered as "the one man who was largely responsible for this great revival movement of our American Heritage blown and pressed glass ...."

MRS. WRIGHT CARRIES ON, 1970 - 1990

After Si Wright's death in 1969, the responsibility for running the company fell upon his widow, Verna Mae, whom he had fondly nicknamed "Toots" many years earlier. She had been in charge of the office staff and maintained the company's books for some three decades, but she did not have Si's sort of knowledge and experience in glassmaking. Nonetheless, Mrs. Wright was determined to maintain the stature and presence of the L. G. Wright Glass Company. She frequently consulted with employees and sales representatives, but she made her own decisions for the best interests of the company as she saw them.

During this twenty-year period, the L. G. Wright Glass Company continued to market its glassware and other products, using its network of sales representatives. Prior to his death, Si Wright had anticipated the manufacture of some new moulds for various articles which would extend the company's existing lines. Many of these projects were carried out as Botson completed the moulds. Mrs. Wright also had glassware made from old moulds (such as God and Home) which had not been utilized previously, and some of these moulds were from Si Wright's purchase of the old Northwood and Dugan-Diamond moulds in 1939.

Just prior to his death, Wright had been interested in producing custard glass, and Mrs. Wright continued this successful color, adding items to the line. Carnival glass was first in the Wright line in 1972; although Si Wright had been interested in this ware for some time, Carnival glass was not made for the Wright firm during his lifetime.

The first printed Master Catalog had appeared in 1968, and the subsequent Master Catalogs produced under Mrs. Wright's direction in the 1970s and 1980s (together with periodic supplements and various price lists) make it relatively easy to document the glassware products of the L. G. Wright Glass Company during this period.

Custard glass, including some decorated items, and pale blue milk glass had been featured in Wright's 1969 Supplement. Among the custard items were a large bowl and matching small bowl (Wright's 910 and 911) in a design based upon Harry Northwood's c. 1899 Nautilus motif in Ivory glass. Wright's sales materials called these Argonaut (sometimes spelled as "Arganaut"), and many collectors refer to this pattern as Argonaut Shell.

The 1970 Supplement featured several new Argonaut items in custard glass, and the entire Argonaut line was also available in blue opalescent. Another new color, dark cobalt blue, also debuted in the 1970 Supplement with an assortment of some 16 items, ranging from pickle jars, goblets and compotes to a fairy lamp and a rose bowl. Some crystal pieces (such as single goblets from the 77-series) were also back in stock in 1970, and Wright's Thistle items in crystal were quite popular in the marketplace.

The Thistle line was extended with new articles throughout the 1970s. The expansion had begun in 1969 when Red Roetteis showed an old Panelled Thistle butterdish to Si Wright, and he became enthusiastic about developing this pattern line. After Si Wright's death, Mrs. Wright continued to invest in Thistle moulds (made by Albert Botson), and new items, some bearing a representation of the old Higbee trademark (a bee with the letters HIG on the wings and body), appeared regularly in the 1970s. Thistle was soon the company's best seller in crystal.

The Wright 1971 Supplement introduced more than two dozen articles in "vaseline ware," a color that had not been made for Wright for several years. A few pieces were also available as acid-finished "vaseline satin," and the 1971 Supplement also shows some items in amber satin, blue satin, green satin, pink satin and ruby satin.

A new item, the L. G. Wright Emblem Plate, was featured on the first page of the 1971 Supplement. This oval plate depicted the rustic outbuilding on the family farm which had served as the first "warehouse" for Wright glass in the 1930s. These satin-finished crystal Emblem Plates were dated 1971 (the Emblem Plate is also known in plain crystal with no date). The year was later changed to 1972, and the Emblem Plate was then available in satin-finished amber. For 1973, the Emblem Plate was offered in satin-finished blue.

Wright's Thistle line from 1972-73 catalog.

An old Dugan pattern called Maple Leaf by collectors was displayed in Wright's 1972 Catalog Supplement. Except for the toothpick holder (a new mould made by Botson), all of Wright's No. 42 Maple Leaf items were made from the original moulds which had been acquired by Wright in 1939; several of these were repaired by Botson in the late 1960s or early 1970s, so the company was interested in offering a number of articles at the same time. The 1972 Catalog Supplement showed Wright's Maple Leaf in crystal, cobalt blue and amberina, and the 1974 Supplement pictured the four-piece table set and a tumbler in Carnival glass.

The second Wright Master Catalog appeared in 1973. The many satin colors introduced a year earlier were absent, but two full pages were devoted to Wright's custard glass, which had sold well since its introduction in 1969. A good deal of ruby and cranberry glassware was shown, including three full pages of cranberry lamps (Wright did not differentiate between cranberry and cranberry opalescent). Most of the cranberry items were the Wright mainstays (barber bottles, cruets, milk pitchers, sugar shakers, tumblers and water pitchers), all of which had been in the line for years.

The brief 1974 Supplement displayed a new Wright trade-mark on its cover. The underlined capital W within a circle can also be found on some glassware items. Wright's No. 7 line (the Cherry pattern) was available in crystal with red and green decoration accented by brilliant gold.

The 1975 Supplement displayed some new milk glass articles decorated with Gold Floral or Woodrose, but the most significant introduction was more Carnival glass, including the God and Home water set and a number of pieces in the Stork and Rushes pattern. All of these were made from the original Dugan moulds (except for the Stork and Rushes sugar cover). The God and Home water set was made in dark Carnival glass only, but the Stork and Rushes pieces were also available in marigold Carnival glass as well as pale blue milk glass and satin-finished crystal.

In the 1976 Supplement, two new Carnival glass items were shown; both the Pony 9" plate and crimped bowl were made from an original Dugan mould. Two new colors were available,

vaseline opalescent and an overlay color, Wildrose Satin (this should not be confused with the earlier Peach Blow).

Wright's Carnival glass offerings were extended further in the 1977 Supplement, as more items were available in dark Carnival glass, which was called Purple Carnival. The Dahlia water pitcher, an old Dugan mould, was shown in Ice Blue Carnival and White Carnival as well as Purple Carnival. Two old Northwood items offered by Wright for years, the Pump and Trough, were now displayed in Purple Slag along with several items from the Cherry line (these were made for Wright by Imperial).

The ranks of the overlay colors were lengthened in 1977 by these: Amber Overlay, Amethyst Overlay, Lt. Blue Overlay and Dk. Blue Overlay. Both Carnival glass and the overlay colors were well represented in Wright's 1978 Supplement, and two new colors, a blue opalescent called Blue Opal and Ruby Slag (made by Imperial) made their debuts.

The 1979 Supplement showed a number of Wright's covered animal dishes in Purple Slag, and the large covered Turkey (based on an early Cambridge piece) was available in amethyst/milk glass combinations as well as in Carnival glass. The Iris pitcher and tumbler (both made from old Dugan moulds) were added in Carnival glass. Wright's Fern pattern (based on Northwood's Daisy and Fern from the 1890s) had been well-known in cranberry opalescent, but the 1979 Supplement added blue opalescent and vaseline opalescent (these were called Blue Fern and Vaseline Fern, respectively).

The 1980 Supplement featured Christmas Snowflake on its front cover, and this motif was available in nearly a dozen cobalt blue opalescent items as well as several cranberry opalescent articles. Three new Carnival glass colors—Ice Green, Ice Pink and Ruby Carnival—were shown, and a few items were available in each hue.

Wright's Mary Gregory decoration on cobalt blue debuted in the firm's 1981 Supplement, and some custard glass was shown with handpainted Gold Floral or Strawberry decorations. An interesting new spot mould motif, Eye Dot and Daisy, was shown in a blue opalescent water set.

Text continued on page 47.

The L. G. Wright Glass Company
New Martinsville, W. Va. 26155

CARNIVAL

12-2
Grape Vine
Lattice Tumbler

800-3
Rambler Rose
Tumbler

8-2
Floral & Grape
Tumbler

12-1
Grape Vine Lattice
Water Pitcher

800-4
Rambler Rose
Water Pitcher

8-1
Floral & Grape Water Pitcher

9-2
Banded Grape
Tumbler

9-1
Banded Grape
Water Pitcher

4-2
Grape Wine

4-1
Grape Decanter

70-8
7" Hen

PURPLE SLAG

24-1
Sweetheart Cherry 7" Rd. Bowl

7-16
Cherry 10" Oval Bowl

7-17
Cherry 5" Oval Bowl

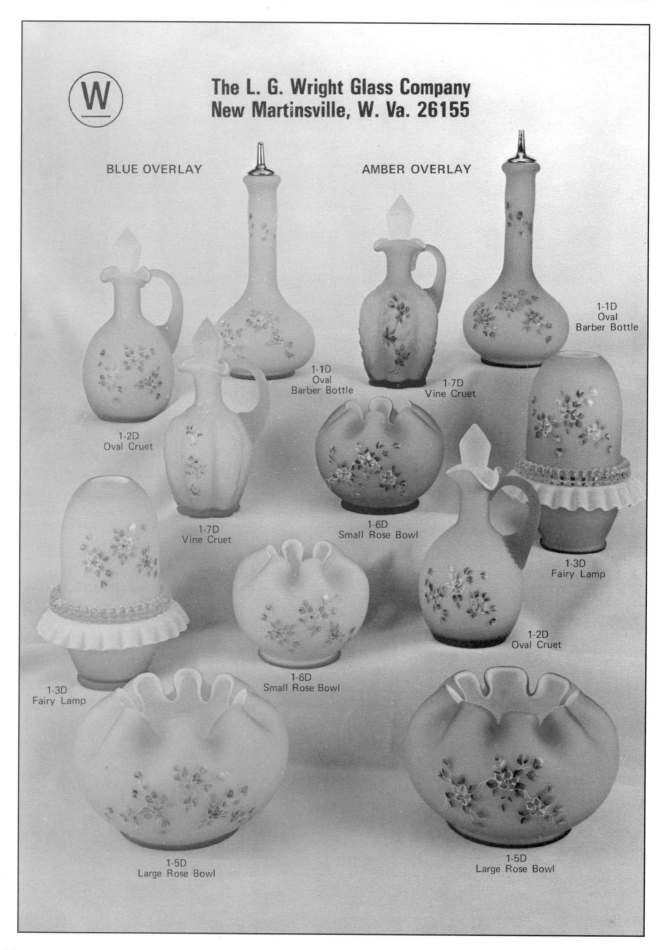

The L. G. Wright Glass Company
New Martinsville, W. Va. 26155

BLUE OVERLAY

AMBER OVERLAY

1-1D
Oval
Barber Bottle

1-2D
Oval Cruet

1-7D
Vine Cruet

1-1D
Oval
Barber Bottle

1-7D
Vine Cruet

1-6D
Small Rose Bowl

1-1D
Oval
Barber Bottle

1-3D
Fairy Lamp

1-3D
Fairy Lamp

1-6D
Small Rose Bowl

1-2D
Oval Cruet

1-5D
Large Rose Bowl

1-5D
Large Rose Bowl

The L. G. Wright Glass Company
New Martinsville, W. Va. 26155

AMETHYST OVERLAY

1-12D
Pickle Jar w/cov.

1-14D
Spooner

1-15D
Fluted Cruet

1-16D
Rd. Cruet

1-17D
Fluted Barber Bottle

1-8D
Vine Salt & Pepper

1-9D
Sugar Shaker

1-10D
Milk Pitcher

1-11D
Tall Cream

1-6D
Small Rose Bowl

1-7D
Vine Cruet

1-3D
Fairy Lamp

1-1D
Oval Barber Bottle

1-2D
Oval Cruet

1980 Supplement
To Master Catalog

EARLY AMERICAN
L.G. WRIGHT

The L. G. Wright Glass Co. New Martinsville, West Virginia 26155

The Mary Gregory decorations consisted of either a boy or a girl, depicted full figure and in profile. The white decoration contrasts very nicely with the dark cobalt glass. This decoration began when sales representative Don Jennings (who also operated Jennings Red Barn in New Martinsville) brought a Mary Gregory item to Wright's decorating department and asked the decorators to match it.

The year 1982 saw a new L. G. Wright Glass Co. Master Catalog, but most of the new articles pictured were hand-painted lamps, including two in Burmese glass. Articles from the Cherry pattern were available in a new slag color, Caramel Slag (made by Imperial), and Wright's covered animal dishes were displayed in both Caramel Slag and Red Slag (formerly known as Ruby Slag).

Instead of a Supplement for 1983, the Wright firm issued two color sheets, captioned "1983 New Items" and "1983 Discontinued Items," each of which was printed on both sides. A new floral decoration (called simply White Floral) was developed for cobalt blue glass, but the main attraction was fourteen items in a new color, Chocolate glass. These ranged from novelties and covered animals dishes to seven articles in Wright's Argonaut line.

A sheet captioned "New Items for 1984" shows the God and Home water set and eleven covered animal dishes in Blue Slag as well as an assortment of Maple Leaf articles in green opalescent called Green Opal. These were made by the Westmoreland Glass Company, and similar Blue Slag was later produced for Wright by the Mosser Glass Company and the Plum Glass Company.

About this same time, the Gibson Glass Company began to produce some blown glass "slag" and "spatter" wares for Wright. These included several of the cruets (vine, fluted, oval and round) which were made decades ago in cranberry glass as well a cream and sugar set, a sugar shaker and a rose bowl. Gibson also made two sizes of paperweights and birds in the slag and spatter treatments, both of which were popular additions to the Wright line.

Among the new items for 1985 were some lamps and Prairie Rose decorated milk glass pieces. A spiral-bound price list detailed the entire Wright line, and a single color sheet showed the discontinued items. In mid-1986, a two-page listing offered "sale" items in Cherry, Daisy and Button, Eye-Winker, and Moon and Star along with selections of other patterns and individual items in a wide variety of colors.

From 1987 to 1989, the L. G. Wright Glass Co. continued to issue yearly price lists keyed to its last Master Catalog, which had been issued in 1982. As one would expect, regular orders from standing accounts and the sales of discontinued items combined to reduce the total number of pieces in the line.

After a long illness, Verna Mae "Toots" Wright died on Sunday, April 1, 1990. Services were held at Iams Funeral Home on April 4, the Rev. James Shepherd officiating. Mrs. Wright was buried next to her husband in New Martinsville's Northview Cemetery. In accordance with her will, the L. G. Wright Glass Company was bequeathed to her cousin, Dorothy Stephan, and to Dorothy's daughter, Phyllis Stephan Buettner. Despite many difficulties, Mrs. Wright had carried on the business for more than two decades after her husband's sudden death.

In a letter to "Our Valued Customers and Friends," Dorothy and Phyllis noted that Verna Mae had "worked hard to continue this business until her untimely death." They pledged to maintain the operations of the L. G. Wright Glass Co. and took several immediate steps to keep in contact with customers. A new price list was developed and mailed to all accounts, and a toll-free 800 number was established. Their letter concluded with this thought: "We know the greatest way to remember Mrs. Wright is to continue the business she worked so diligently to maintain."

L. G. WRIGHT GLASS IN THE 1990s

When Dorothy Stephan and her daughter, Phyllis Stephan Buettner, inherited the L. G. Wright Glass Company, they faced a formidable task, namely, the need to learn all they could about the business as soon as possible. Dorothy had prepared the company's weekly payrolls for some time, so she was familiar with that area, but neither Dorothy nor Phyllis, who had a career in hospital administration, knew much about glassmaking or the company's accounts.

They felt "overwhelmed," but they plunged right in, determined to operate the L. G. Wright Glass Company. The Wright Master Catalogs and various Supplements gave them a quick overview of the line. Conversations with long-time employees helped pinpoint the best-selling items and identify important relationships with glass manufacturers and suppliers of lamp parts and other necessities. The daily mail—containing orders, questions and correspondence—provided details about customers and sales representatives. Trips to trade shows in Chicago and Pittsburgh were valuable for making contacts and learning about the glass industry.

Phyllis worked in the Wright retail gift shop on some weekends, too, just to hear what the browsers and purchasers were saying and to understand their interests. On one occasion, she discovered a $10 undercharge to one customer who had left hours ago with a purchase of Wright glass. Phyllis had "chalked it up to experience," but the customer discovered the mistake and returned during the next week to pay the $10 to avoid trouble for "the new girl that was here last Saturday."

In August, 1990, the L. G. Wright Glass Co. released a one-page price list of items that were now back in stock. A few pieces of Maple Leaf were listed in cobalt blue, and there were a number of crystal items in Beaded, Daisy and Button, Eye-Winker and Moon and Star as well as decorated crystal pieces in the Cherry pattern.

Dorothy and Phyllis had decided that relatively small crystal items (some of which could be decorated) were the best first steps in maintaining the Wright line. These pieces were made by the Wilkerson Glass Co. in nearby Moundsville.

Wright's decorators soon learned how to paint the Cherry pieces, and decorated Sweetheart articles debuted later.

In September, 1990, the L. G. Wright Glass Co. issued a completely new catalog with color photos of its glassware and an attractive Victorian-style silhouette on the front cover. Many crystal items were available in the Thistle pattern, and quite a few of the firm's other distinctive patterns (Daisy and Button, Eye-Winker, Moon and Star, etc.) were represented along with many novelty items. In general, not much colored glass was represented, but there were some articles in cranberry (including the 84-1 and 84-2 water pitchers) and a few individual items, such as the Wildrose wine, could be ordered in several colors. No Carnival glass was listed, but the Slag and Spatter pieces made for Wright by the Gibson enterprise continued to be popular.

A lengthy list of new items was ready in January, 1991, and it extended most of the patterns from the previous list. In addition, more than a dozen Daisy and Button items were available in pink; several were also listed in cobalt blue along with some animal dishes. New Ice Pink items ranged from Thistle pattern articles to Hen covered dishes and two sizes of slippers. Five covered animal dishes—including three sizes of Hens, the Dog and the Frog—were available in black glass, the first time this color was offered by Wright. These were produced for Wright by the Summit Art Glass Company.

For 1992-93 and again in 1994, the Wright firm used a printed double-pocket folder to display its wares. Some of the pages and color photos were taken from the 1991 catalog because these items were still in stock, but other photos or pages were revised added to reflect additions to the line. Among the additions were crystal versions of the Squirrel candy box (70-7) and the large covered Turkey (70-17) along with several items of Daisy and Button.

In June, 1994, a letter to Wright customers announced that an updated catalog and price list were in preparation. In anticipation of some price changes, the company offered sale prices (5-10% off) on orders placed before August 15,

Dorothy Stephan posed with a decorated lamp for a newspaper story about Wright glass in the early 1990s.

1994. This same letter carried the good news that some Amethyst Carnival glass items were back "in stock" and mentioned these items: Peacock bowl, Stork and Rushes bowl, and the God and Home pitcher and tumbler.

Also in 1994, a new price list was issued on October 1, and it was intended to cover the 1995 year. The decorated milk glass items (apothecary jars, candy boxes and vases) were available in many different motifs, and decorated lamps could be ordered from a list of more than sixty different patterns. Several Sweetheart pattern items were available in crystal or crystal decorated with gold, and the large Sweetheart bowl was pictured in Cobalt Carnival. Sweetheart is a c. 1905 Dugan motif originally called Victor, but it was called Jewelled Heart for years by glass collectors who misattributed it to Harry Northwood.

Some crystal Moon and Star items were added to the selection, and three Moon and Star items were listed in ruby along with several in Panel Grape. All of Wright's crystal glassware was available in four tinted colors: Stormy Blue, Sparkling Grape, Lemon Yellow and Marigold. Like the previous Ice Pink in 1990-91, these were created with a "lustre" process wherein special chemicals are applied to the glass by Wright employees, and the pieces are placed in a decorating kiln to bond the color.

The 1996 Wright catalog featured crystal pattern glass items (in Thistle, Daisy and Button, Eye-Winker, Moon and Star, Westward Ho, and Three Face) as well as many decorated and colored articles. One full page shows Amethyst Carnival glass (including the God and Home water set), and many decorated milk glass lamps are pictured.

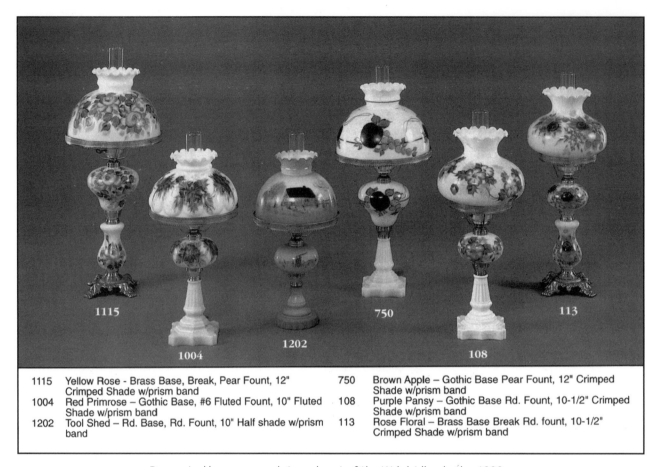

1115	Yellow Rose - Brass Base, Break, Pear Fount, 12" Crimped Shade w/prism band	750	Brown Apple – Gothic Base Pear Fount, 12" Crimped Shade w/prism band
1004	Red Primrose – Gothic Base, #6 Fluted Fount, 10" Fluted Shade w/prism band	108	Purple Pansy – Gothic Base Rd. Fount, 10-1/2" Crimped Shade w/prism band
1202	Tool Shed – Rd. Base, Rd. Fount, 10" Half shade w/prism band	113	Rose Floral – Brass Base Break Rd. fount, 10-1/2" Crimped Shade w/prism band

Decorated lamps are an integral part of the Wright line in the 1990s.

In October, 1996, the L. G. Wright Glass Company opened a museum adjacent to its gift shop at the plant. More than 300 pieces are on display in the museum, and they reflect the nearly six decades that the Wright firm has been in business. A group of glass aficionados called the West Virginia Glass Gathering visited the museum shortly after it opened, and one longtime collector was heard to exclaim "I never dreamed all of this was Wright glass!" Now, because of this book, even more glass collectors will learn about Wright glass.

THE WRIGHT LINE

Unlike the plants which manufactured and sold their own glass lines, the L. G. Wright Glass Company did not bring out new patterns, colors or decorations on a yearly basis. A Wright pattern line (such as Panel Grape or Moon and Star) or an item (such as the Pump and Trough) which continued to sell reasonably well would be made in various colors from time to time and, thus, could remain in the line for many years.

Since Wright owned the moulds from which his items were made, he was free to transport the moulds from one factory to another. Records kept at the Viking Glass Company in New Martinsville show that some Wright moulds remained at Viking for several years while others came from Paden City to Viking for a short time and then were taken to Fenton or Fostoria or Westmoreland, only to return to Viking later.

In order to keep track of the whereabouts of its various moulds and the quantities of glass being made, the Wright firm maintained a card file, especially during the busy 1960s. Each mould was numbered beginning with "W-1". These same numbers were actually put on the moulds themselves, too (however, these mould numbers bear no relationship to the numbering system used after 1962 for ordering glass). The card file contained a card for each numbered mould as well as information about its factory location and, if applicable, the amount of glass made with it year by year.

Wright typically had glass made in relatively small quantities. He bought by the "turn" or (even half-turn), and this might mean 175 blown cranberry water pitchers or several hundred of a small pressed piece. A document dated October 25, 1938, from the New Martinsville Glass Co. calls for half-turns each of baskets, goblets, hats, plates and slippers in four different colors (amber, blue, crystal and vaseline) as well as a note to "work Lion goblet 1 hour."

When Wright's inventory of a particular item was getting low, he would make the rounds of the glass plants which could make the ware, typically contracting for a few turns wherever the price was best. "Si was a shrewd businessman," Frank M. Fenton recalls. "My father [Frank L. Fenton] often made glass for him at prices barely over cost because he wanted to keep our skilled workers busy during a slack period. I refigured the prices quoted to Wright in the mid-fifties as we learned more about our actual costs. We were changing the pricing structure on our regular line at the same time. But, Si still had us make a lot of glass for him."

Getting pressed items made in the standard glass colors—amber, amethyst, blue, green, and ruby—was not particularly difficult in the 1940s, as Wright could turn to Fenton, Fostoria, Paden City, Westmoreland or Viking. Each of these plants quoted prices to Si Wright, some even updating their quotes regularly in small binders (many of Fenton's quote books are preserved at the plant in Williamstown). When the color varied a bit from factory to factory or batch to batch, this was not a major concern to Wright.

When Paden City closed in the early 1950s, Wright's choices among manufacturers were limited somewhat, but, when new glass companies opened—such as the Mosser firm in Cambridge, Ohio—Wright had another potential supplier, especially for the smaller items in pressed ware. When Fostoria and Viking closed in the 1980s, the Wright firm dealt with Dalzell-Viking and established relationships with the Mosser Glass Company and the Summit Art Glass Company. More recently, the Gibson Glass Company and the Wilkerson Glass Co. have made Wright ware.

If Wright needed a particular color (pink, custard or vaseline) or wanted a special treatment (opalescent glass or Carnival glass) his choices were constrained because not all factories made such ware regularly or had workers with the skills necessary to produce the ware successfully. This was especially true with blown glass, so Wright typically went to Fenton for this type of ware, although Salvatore "Sam" Diana's Venetian Glass Corp. in Rochester, Pa., made some cranberry and "Peach Blow" in the 1950s and 1960s.

Blown milk glass lamp parts were made for Wright by the Davis-Lynch Glass Company of Star City, West Virginia, for many years, although some were also made by the Bailey Glass Company in Morgantown, and Wright may have

EXCLUSIVE GIFTS IN
EARLY AMERICAN
GLASSWARE
AND
COLONIAL LAMPS OF
YESTERYEAR

Advertising flyer from the mid-1960s.

done a little business with the Rodefer Glass Co. in Bellaire, Ohio. Davis-Lynch also decorated glassware (especially lamps) for Wright, and the Wright decorating shop was started in 1968 when Si Wright hired Gloria "Ticky" Mitchell, a former decorator at Davis-Lynch.

Fostoria produced an excellent pink, and most of Wright's Moon and Star articles or Daisy and Button pieces in this hue were made there. Fenton made opalescent glass regularly and turned out lots of custard glass in the late 1960s. Fenton would not make Carnival glass for Wright, however, so he turned to Westmoreland for this treatment. Westmoreland also made Wright's Chocolate glass in the 1980s.

Some significant American glass companies had little contact with Wright. Heisey, for example, is totally absent from the records at Wright, and the company's contact with Imperial is limited to decorated Cherry pieces in crystal glass and some slag glass pieces. Lucile Kennedy, who worked at Imperial from 1942-1982, recalls that Si Wright came to Imperial in the early 1950s to inquire about getting glass made. Imperial was reviving milk glass, and collectors were concerned that the products were not marked. Imperial President Carl Gustkey had Lucile inform Wright that Imperial could not make glass for him at that time. Si Wright bought Turkeys at Cambridge in the 1930s (and later had a Turkey mould made), but his only other contact with this firm seems to have been the purchase of crystal stoppers for cruets.

The point of this discussion is a simple one, namely, that Wright glass is, by definition and practical fact, glassware made for and sold by the L. G. Wright Glass Company. One cannot look at a given Wright glass item and easily determine the manufacturer. The mould belongs to the L. G. Wright Glass Co., of course, so it follows that the glass is "Wright glass," regardless of its particular place of manufacture. When a few turns of an article were made for Wright, the item might remain in stock for years, so dates are also difficult to establish. Wright generally did not allow other glass plants to use his moulds to produce ware for their own lines.

Prior to the early 1960s, all the various items in the Wright glass line were simply listed and described in typewritten price lists. The sales representatives literally had to "write out" each order, item by item, e. g., "4 doz. Panel Grape goblets, Blue Opalescent," on a simple printed form.

About 1962, a numbering system for customer orders was put into place to simplify the process. The major patterns were assigned numbers, e. g., Daisy and Button (22), Moon and Star (44), Panel Grape (55), Three Face (65), and Westward Ho (66). The number 77 was used for all the "miscellaneous" patterns, each of which contained only a few articles, along with many different novelties and individual goblets.

Each article within a given pattern line was assigned its own number, too, and these followed the pattern number: e. g., 44-22 is the Moon and Star goblet; 55-3 is the Panel Grape 6" covered compote; and 66-5 is the Westward Ho wine (interestingly, the superstitious Wrights avoided using the numeral "13" throughout the system!).

Other items were grouped by type. The number 70 was reserved for covered candy boxes, and 80 designated animal candy boxes (these are now commonly called covered dishes by collectors). The various blown barber bottles, creams, cruets, milk pitchers, sugar shakers and water pitchers—in the line almost continuously since the 1930s—were given numbers from 84 to 99. Some patterns and items appear in two places in the Wright numbering system. Maize, for example, is listed as pattern 40, but a few items also appear in the vases and rose bowls classification, designated 75.

Previous books which offer information on Wright glass (such as Hammond's *Confusing Collectibles* and *Identifying Pattern Glass Reproductions* by Jenks, Luna and Reilly) do little to explain the full history of Wright glassware. *Identifying Pattern Glass Reproductions*, for example, relies all too heavily upon catalogs from the late 1960s and thereafter, thus ignoring the full scope of Wright's earliest wares as well as his expanding line and increasing sales in the 1940s and 1950s. Consequently, *Identifying Pattern Glass Reproductions* fails to note some L. G. Wright colors and omits many glassware products which are of interest to today's collectors.

The remainder of this chapter lists the entire Wright line, following the numbering system begun in the early 1960s. Information about the probable dates of manufacture is given, but readers must bear in mind that items went in and out

1963   THE L. G. WRIGHT GLASS COMPANY
                New Martinsville, W. Va.

PHONE: 304-455-2630

Terms: 1% 15 days from date of invoice,
       Net 30 days.
       No discount on parcel post shipments.
       No charge for packing or cartons.
       F. O. B. New Martinsville, W. Va.

Claims: Must be filed by consignee.
        Examine contents of packages carefully,
        small items can easily be discarded
        with packing material.

Returns: Not accepted without our consent to
         return.

Prices: Subject to change without notice.

Orders: Subject to approval of home office.

1963   THE L. G. WRIGHT GLASS COMPANY
                New Martinsville, W. Va.

Page 2

CHERRY PATTERN

1963

A-Amber   AM-Amethyst   R-Ruby
B-Blue   AR-Amberina   S-Slag
G-Green   VA-Vaseline

Item No.		Price Each
7-1	Bowl Footed Large Shallow, Regular A. B. G. AM. AR.	$ 4.75 5.75
7-2	Butter and Cover A. G. AR.	2.00 2.50
7-3	Compote 6" Open Scroll A. G. S.	1.25 1.50
7-4	Cream Pitcher A. B. G. VA. AR. R. S.	1.25 1.50
7-5	Sugar Vase A. B. G. VA. AR. R. S.	1.25 1.50
7-6	Salt Dip A. B. G. AM. AR.	.75 .95
7-7	Salver Large Ftd. A. B. G. AM. AR.	4.75 5.75
7-8	Toothpick A. B. G. AM. AR. R.	.55 .70
7-9	Tumbler A. B.	1.05
7-10	Water Pitcher A. B.	3.75

NO. 7 CHERRY PATTERN

7-4 CHERRY PATTERN CREAM Amber, Blue, Green, Vaseline, Amberina, Ruby, Slag

7-5 CHERRY PATTERN SUGAR Amber, Blue, Green, Vaseline, Amberina, Ruby, Slag

7-10 CHERRY WATER PITCHER Amber, Blue

7-1 CHERRY LARGE FOOTED BOWL REGULAR ALSO SHALLOW Amber, Blue, Green, Amethyst, Amberina

of the line. When the date for a new mould, usually by Albert Botson, is known, it is given.

EPERGNES

In the early 1940s, Joe Weishar's Island Mould and Machine Co. made the moulds for L. G. Wright's large pressed epergne, which consists of a large central cone and three smaller cones—all of which are mounted in a glass fitting attached with a metal peg to a large base. The inspiration for these was Harry Northwood's No. 305 Flower Stand, which was marketed from his Wheeling factory in 1906.

Wright arranged for Fenton to make the pressed epergne in several crest treatments (Aqua Crest, Gold Crest, Rose Crest, opal with amethyst crest, amethyst with opal crest, and blue with crystal crest) as well as blue opalescent and vaseline opalescent. During World War II and into the 1950s, many of these epergnes were sold to the Koscherak Brothers, Inc., a New York City importer.

In the 1940s and early 1950s, Fenton also made two blown epergnes for L. G. Wright, and

ANTIQUE GLASS REPRODUCTIONS
of Authentic Design

EPERGNE
with four vases. Height 17″, diam. of Bowl 11″.

62/21B Opalescent Blue	Each	**$11.75**
62/21C Transparent Crystal	Each	11.75
62/32 Milk Glass, Blue edges	Each	12.75

We present a collection of recognized Old American glass designs eagerly sought by collectors, hand made and finished from old moulds—in rare Opalescent Blue, Milk Glass and Crystal.

these were often resold to A. A. Sales in St. Louis, another firm which had specialized in imported glass. These have a single cone which fits into the base, and they were made in Fenton's ruby overlay (Wright called this Cranberry) as well as Peach Blow and Snow Crest (cranberry with opal crest).

NO. 3 BEADED

Having purchased the old Northwood mould for the No. 562 rose bowl (see *Harry Northwood: The Early Years*, p. 134) in 1939, Wright used it as the basis for both a footed compote and an ivy bowl. In mid-1960, he also had a new mould made to create the 3-3 large footed bowl; these were flared or crimped (Wright liked to call them "crimpt"). When made with a different plunger, the smaller items were marketed as candleholders (3-1) and, combined with a Beaded large ivy bowl (3-5), sold as the 3-6 three-piece console set.

In 1990-91, all the Beaded items were made in crystal. The 3-1 and 3-2 pieces were also made in the "Stormy Blue" and "Sparkling Ruby" lustres about 1995.

3-1 small footed candleholder
3-2 small footed compote
3-3 large footed bowl (crimpt or flared)
3-4 small footed ivy bowl
3-5 large ivy bowl.
3-6 three-piece console set

NO. 5 BEADED GRAPE

This was another early Wright line, and all of these pieces (plus the salt/pepper shakers which were soon out of the line) appear in inventories or price lists from the late 1940s or early 1950s. Both the goblet and the square plate were shown in retail catalogs issued by the John Marshall Company for 1949-50. The items listed below were still in the line in the mid-1960s.

5-1 square covered compote
5-2 oil bottle or cruet
5-3 goblet
5-4 8″ square plate
5-5 4″ square nappy or sauce dish

NO. 7 CHERRY

In 1939, Wright acquired several c. 1911 Dugan moulds for this pattern (now called Wreathed Cherry by many collectors) from Indiana, Pa. The Cherry cream and open sugar bowl with crimped top were in the Wright line by

3-6 Beaded three-piece console set.

late 1939 and are illustrated in blue opalescent in a Koscherak Bros. brochure from the mid-1940s along with a basket made from the sugar. In the 1950s and 1960s, the Cherry line was extended when a few new moulds were made.

In the mid-1970s, a number of Cherry items were available in crystal with bright gold and red and green decorations; these were made and decorated for Wright by the Imperial Glass Co. at Bellaire. Imperial also made Purple Slag and Ruby Slag pieces for Wright in 1977-78 as well as a few Caramel Slag items in the early 1980s. Beginning in 1990-91, Cherry pieces were made in crystal by the Wilkerson Glass Co. and decorated by the Wright decorating staff in New Martinsville.

7-1 large footed fruit bowl
7-2 butter and cover
7-3 6" open compote [also known as Cherry Scroll]
7-4 cream pitcher
7-5 sugar vase (usually made crimpt)
7-6 salt dip (Botson mould 1960)
7-7 large footed salver
7-8 toothpick (Botson mould 1959)
7-9 tumbler
7-10 or 7-14 large water pitcher (Botson mould 1958)
7-12 goblet (Botson mould 1966)
7-15 ice tea
7-16 10" oval bowl
7-17 5" oval bowl

NO. 11 DOUBLE WEDDING RING

This pattern dates from the early 1960s (all the moulds made by Botson), and it was gradually extended to include the articles listed below.

11-1 6" covered compote
11-2 goblet
11-3 4" covered jelly
11-4 8" round plate
11-5 sherbet
11-6 toothpick
11-7 wine
11-8 salt dip
11-9 footed tumbler

NO. 22 DAISY AND BUTTON

Like Panel Grape and Moon and Star, this is

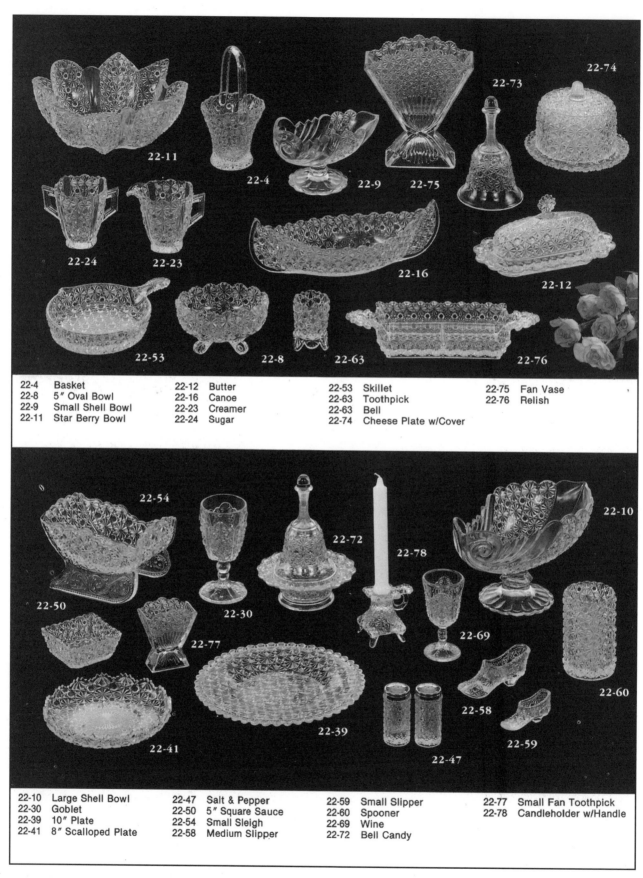

22-4	Basket	22-12	Butter	22-53	Skillet	22-75	Fan Vase
22-8	5" Oval Bowl	22-16	Canoe	22-63	Toothpick	22-76	Relish
22-9	Small Shell Bowl	22-23	Creamer	22-63	Bell		
22-11	Star Berry Bowl	22-24	Sugar	22-74	Cheese Plate w/Cover		

22-10	Large Shell Bowl	22-47	Salt & Pepper	22-59	Small Slipper	22-77	Small Fan Toothpick
22-30	Goblet	22-50	5" Square Sauce	22-60	Spooner	22-78	Candleholder w/Handle
22-39	10" Plate	22-54	Small Sleigh	22-69	Wine		
22-41	8" Scalloped Plate	22-58	Medium Slipper	22-72	Bell Candy		

one of the L. G. Wright Glass Company's most extensive and successful patterns. However, the Daisy and Button line also includes quite a few novelty items (such as hats, slippers and sleighs) which serve to increase the size of the line well beyond the ranks of utilitarian pieces.

The Wright Daisy and Button line includes some items (22-30 goblet, 22-37 water pitcher and 22-69 wine) which can be classified as the pattern Daisy and Button with Thumbprint Panels (crystal examples may be decorated with amber or ruby stain).

In addition to the hats and slippers, goblets and plates were among Wright's earliest products, dating from the late 1930s. Some items, such as the 22-11 star-shaped berry bowl and 22-51 5" star-shaped sauce, were based on articles popularized by the famous Hobbs, Brockunier and Company of Wheeling in the 1880s.

Several Daisy and Button items were originated and discontinued before the early 1960s and are not included among Wright's numbered pieces: bone tray; cheese dish; Boat ash tray; wall planter; mustard with wire handle; Anvil ash tray; and 4" Sandal.

During the 1950s and 1960s, Wright's Daisy and Button items were made in a wide variety of colors, including amber, amberina, amethyst, blue, green, pink, ruby and vaseline. In 1990-91, about a dozen Daisy and Button items were made in crystal, and many of the same articles were produced in pink for 1991.

22-1 cart ash tray
22-2 small fan ash tray
22-3 6" square ash tray
22-4 handled basket
22-5 6" crimpt or flared bowl
22-6 11" footed bowl, crimpt
22-7 10" oval bowl, four-toed
22-8 5" oval bowl, four-toed
22-9 13" salad bowl (sold with 22-38 and wooden fork and spoon)
22-10 large Shell footed bowl
22-11 11" star-shaped berry bowl
22-12 oval ["rectangular" is more descriptive] butter and cover
22-14 5" oval candleholder, four-toed
22-15 miniature stove candleholder
22-16 11½" canoe
22-17 4" covered compote
22-18 6" oval covered compote, four-toed
22-19 6" large square covered compote
22-20 6" round covered compote
22-21 large cream
22-22 covered sugar
22-23 small cream, square
22-24 small sugar, square

22-25 cruet
22-26 punch cup
22-27 finger bowl
22-28 flower bowl w/block
22-29 goblet (plain stem)
22-30 goblet, T. P. [Thumbprint] panel.
22-31 Gypsy Kettle w/cover and spoon
22-32 medium hat
22-33 small hat
22-34 honey dish and cover
22-35 6½" handled nappy
22-36 pickle jar w/metal cover
22-37 water pitcher
22-38 17" plate (sold with 22-9 and wooden fork and spoon)
22-39 10" plate
22-40 7" round plate
22-41 8" round scalloped plate
22-42 15 pc. punch set (composed of 22-9 13" salad bowl, 22-38 17" plate, a dozen 22-26 punch cups and a ladle)
22-43 punch set (same as 22-42, but lacks the plate and has hooks for the cups)
22-44 rose bowl
22-45 round salt dip
22-46 triangle salt dip
22-47 salt and pepper shakers
22-48 13" footed salver
22-49 4" round sauce
22-50 4" square sauce
22-51 5" star sauce
22-52 square footed sherbet
22-53 skillet (Botson mould 1960)
22-54 small sleigh
22-55 small sleigh w/candleholder
22-56 large sleigh
22-57 Kitten slipper
22-58 medium slipper
22-59 small slipper
22-60 spooner or vase
22-61 stick candy jar
22-62 fan-shaped toothpick
22-63 round toothpick
22-64 triangle toothpick (Botson mould 1960)
22-65 large fan tray
22-66 three-part relish tray, 7" long
22-67 9 oz. tumbler
22-68 8" footed vase, square
22-69 wine, T. P. [Thumbprint] panel
22-70 bell candy box
22-71 6½" bon bon

Daisy and Button lamps.

22-72 small Shell footed bowl
22-73 bell w/clapper

NO. 25 EYE-WINKER

This pattern is based upon an 1890s motif popularized by the Dalzell, Gilmore and Leighton Company of Findlay, Ohio. Wright's Eye-Winker debuted with seven items in 1963-64, and the line grew to thirty articles by 1968. All of these moulds were probably made at Albert Botson's B. Machine and Mould Co. in Cambridge, Ohio, and there are invoices for many of them in the Wright archives. In 1990-91, half a dozen Eye-Winker articles were being made in crystal.

25-1 6" covered compote
25-2 7½" covered compote
25-3 goblet
25-4 sherbet
25-5 4" sauce
25-7 wine
25-8 7" ash tray
25-9 4½" ash tray
25-10 10" footed bowl
25-11 5" four-toed bowl
25-12 butter and cover

Pure Honey, Satin Glass and a Black Cherry Dipper

Remember mom's hot biscuits dripping with sweet honey? Well, we Forslunds sure do. And now we can all relive those delicious memories with Pure Wildflower Honey packaged in a beautiful 12 oz. Eye Winker Jar of satin glass, sealed with natural beeswax. So you won't miss a drop, we've also included an old-fashioned wooden honey dipper. (Still the only practical way to handle honey). It's handturned with care from wild black cherry. Add a 16 oz. jar for refills and you've got a Christmas gift that will be thoroughly enjoyed by young and old alike! $25.00

25-5	4" Rd. Sauce – Crystal	25-28	6" Vase – Crystal
25-23	Toothpick – Crystal	25-25	Marmalade w/cover – Crystal
25-19	Eye Winker Sugar – Crystal	25-20	Eye Winker Honey – Crystal
25-18	Eye Winker Cream – Crystal	25-3	Goblet – Crystal
25-22	Salt Dip – Crystal	25-27	Tumbler – Crystal
25-11	Soap Dish – Crystal	25-26	Water Pitcher – Crystal
		25-29	Fairy Lamp – 1 Pink, 1 Cobalt
		25-17	5" Open Compote – Amber

25-14 4" covered compote
25-15 low footed 5" covered compote
25-16 high footed 6" open compote
25-17 5" open compote
25-18 cream
25-19 sugar and cover
25-20 honey dish and cover
25-21 pickle tray
25-22 salt dip
25-23 toothpick
25-24 salt and pepper shakers
25-25 marmalade and cover
25-26 pitcher
25-27 tumbler
25-28 6" vase
25-29 fairy lamp
25-30 8" vase

NO. 33 HOBNAIL

There were many Hobnail or Dew Drop patterns in the 1880s, and Wright surely knew of these. The barber bottle was first made in the 1930s and was among Wright's earliest pieces and marks the outset of his company's long relationship with Fenton.

In addition to these items, Wright also had a Hobnail fairy light. These were shown in the 1973 Master Catalog (33-B blue, 33-R ruby, 33-G green and 33-A amber). These moulds were sold to the Viking Glass Co. by Mrs. Wright.

33-1 barber bottle w/stopper
33-2 covered bowl
33-3 small footed compote [made from goblet]
33-4 cream
33-5 open sugar
33-6 cruet
33-7 finger bowl
33-8 goblet
33-9 rose bowl crimpt
33-10 salt and pepper shakers
33-11 tumbler (mould made by Weishar's
    Island Mould and Machine Co. in 1950)

NO. 35 JERSEY SWIRL

This pattern was developed in the late 1950s and early 1960s, and it grew to eleven items in 1968. Invoices in the Wright archives indicate that all these moulds were made by Botson's B. Machine and Mould Co.

35-1 4" covered compote
35-2 high footed 5" covered compote

35-3 low footed 5" covered compote
35-4 footed compote (crimpt)
35-5 goblet
35-6 6" plate
35-7 10" plate
35-8 small salt dip
35-9 master salt dip
35-10 4" footed sauce
35-11 wine

NO. 37 MAGNET AND GRAPE

The moulds for all of the articles in this short line were made by Albert Botson in 1962. Ruth Webb Lee reported articles in Magnet and Grape with Frosted Leaf as early as November, 1941, but these were not Wright products.

37-1 champagne
37-2 goblet
37-3 4" covered jelly
37-4 sherbet
37-5 wine

NO. 40 MAIZE

Based upon an 1889 pattern made at the Libbey Glass Company in Toledo, Ohio, these are among Wright's most interesting items. The moulds were made by Botson's B. Machine and Mould Co. between 1962 and 1966.

These items were usually made in overlay glass colors (amber overlay, blue overlay, dark blue overlay, pink overlay and rose overlay), and they may be found with regular or satin finish. The interior of overlay articles is always opal glass. Some Maize pieces, such as the rose bowl, were also made in cranberry glass. Fenton made most of Wright's Maize, but some articles may have been made by Salvatore "Sam" Diana at his Venetian Glass Corp. in Rochester, Pa.

40-1 covered candy box
40-2 rose bowl
40-3 sugar shaker
40-4 tumbler
40-5 water pitcher
40-6 7" vase
40-7 9" vase
40-8-5 pickle jar

NO. 42 MAPLE LEAF

This was an old Dugan pattern c. 1911, and the moulds were probably in the group bought by L. G. Wright in 1939 (this pattern should not

Maize lamp

42-4 compote
42-5 tumbler
42-6 water pitcher
42-7 spooner
42-8 toothpick
42-9 salver (made from compote)

NO. 44 MOON AND STAR

Based upon a late 1880s pattern called Palace, which was originated by the Adams Glass Co. of Pittsburgh, the L. G. Wright Glass Company's Moon and Star is the firm's longest single line and one of its best-selling.

Moon and Star goblets and bowls appear in the 1938 Wright inventory, and many items were added to the line in the first half of the 1940s. Ruth Webb Lee pictured the goblet, footed sauce dish and egg cup (*American Collector*, March, 1945), and she later mentioned a Moon and Star miniature night lamp (made from the egg cup) in the same publication (October, 1946).

The 1947 Wright inventory lists more than 20 different items, and a Koscherak Brothers brochure shows several in opalescent blue. Most of these moulds were made by Weishar's Island Mould and Machine Co. Additional moulds (made by Botson) allowed Wright to expand the Moon and Star line during the 1950s and 1960s, and more than 50 different articles were listed by 1966.

Neither the syrup pitcher (Botson mould 1959) or the 10-10½" plate appear in Wright's numerical listing, so these were likely discontinued before the early 1960s. There are many Wright lamps which use various Moon and Star items as a shade, and Wright's 1972 Supplement shows the Moon and Star Fairy Lamp in ruby as well as blue and amber (these have crystal inserts to hold the candle).

44-1 8½" ash tray
44-2 butter and cover
44-3 9" candleholder
44-4 6" candleholder (sold with 44-6
    as console set)
44-5 11" console bowl
44-6 8" console bowl (sold with 44-4
    as console set)
44-7 champagne
44-8 4" covered compote
44-9 6" d., tall covered compote
44-10 6" d., low covered compote
44-11 8" covered compote
44-12 6½" open compote crimpt

be confused with Wright's 72-4 compote and 77-29 goblet, which were also called Maple Leaf).

Wright's 1972 Supplement introduced No. 42 Maple Leaf in crystal, cobalt and amberina, and there is evidence that some of these moulds had been repaired by Botson in 1969, the same year he made the toothpick mould. Wright's 1974 Supplement shows five pieces of Maple Leaf in Carnival glass and notes that it was "made from original moulds." All of the Maple Leaf items were made in green opalescent in 1984, and several articles were made in Cobalt Blue and a ruby which often struck as amberina.

42-1 cream
42-2 sugar and cover
42-3 butter and cover

Maple Leaf items in crystal, plus a decorated biscuit jar.

Moon and Star from the 1990s.

44-14 8" medium open compote
44-15 10" large open compote
44-16 large cream (pressed handle)
44-17 cruet
44-18 decanter (Botson mould 1956)
44-19 small epergne
44-20 medium epergne
44-21 finger bowl
44-22 goblet (Botson mould 1959)
44-23 ice tea (Botson mould 1962)
44-24 3¼" jelly with cover
44-25 footed juice glass
44-26 8" plate or salad plate, scalloped edge
44-27 handled relish
44-28 oval relish (Botson mould 1962)
44-29 8" rectangular relish
44-30 salt dip
44-31 salt and pepper shakers
44-32 12" large salver
44-33 10" medium salver
44-34 8" small salver

Moon and Star from the 1990s.

44-35 footed sauce dish
44-36 high foot sherbet
44-37 spoonholder
44-38 large sugar and cover
44-39 toothpick (Botson mould 1964)

This original black-and-white photograph (c. 1950) shows a variety of items in Wright's Moon and Star. **A.** 44-2 butter and cover. **B.** 44-10 6" d., low covered compote. **C.** Un-numbered 10½" large plate. **D.** 44-9 6" d., tall covered compote. **E.** 44-8 4" covered compote. **F.** 44-16 large cream. **G.** 44-38 large sugar and cover. **H.** 44-14 8" medium open compote. **I.** 44-33 10" medium salver. **J.** 44-37 spoonholder. **K.** 44-31 salt and pepper shakers. **L.** 44-21 finger bowl. **M.** 44-34 8" small salver. **N.** 44-26 8" plate or salad plate, scalloped edge. **O.** 44-12 6½" open compote crimpt. **P.** 44-41 footed tumbler. **Q.** 44-7 champagne. **R.** 44-22 goblet. **S.** egg cup (later called 44-25 footed juice glass). **T.** 44-35 footed sauce dish. **U.** 44-30 salt dip.

44-40 13" pickle, relish or celery tray
44-41 footed tumbler
44-42 wine
44-43 6" nappy, flared or crimpt
44-44 rose bowl
44-45 flower bowl with block
44-46 12" bowl, flared or crimpt
44-47 stem covered candy box 6"
44-48 stem open compote 7" flared
44-49 stem open compote 5" flared
44-50 stem high-footed covered jelly 4½"
44-51 13½" plate
44-52 low covered sugar
44-53 5" ash tray
44-54 sugar shaker (Botson mould 1959)

44-55 soap dish
44-56 water pitcher

NO. 55 PANEL GRAPE

This line is likely based on a popular Westmoreland motif which is called Panelled Grape by collectors. Lee mentioned Wright's goblet in mid-1939, and she thought the tumbler was from Czechoslovakia (one of Wright's customers was the Czecho-Slovak Glass Co., an importer based in New York City who also handled American-made reproductions).

Many of Wright's early Moon and Star moulds were made by Weishar's Island Mould and Machine Co. in the 1940s. These include the cus-

This original black-and-white photograph (c. 1950) shows a variety of items in Wright's Panel Grape. **A.** large cream. **B.** large sugar and cover. **C.** 55-9 1 qt. water pitcher. **D.** 55-11 10" plate. **E.** celery vase. **F.** 6" celery vase. **G.** 55-8 4" covered jelly compote. **H.** 55-17 saucer. **I.** 55-6 cup. **J.** 55-12 8" salad plate. **K.** 55-5 small cream/sugar set. **L.** 8" nappy. M. 55-7 goblet. N. footed parfait. **O.** 14 oz. ice tea. **P.** 5" nappy. **Q.** 4" fruit or sauce dish. **R.** 9 oz. water tumbler. **S.** tumbler. **T.** cocktail. **U.** 55-18 sherbet. **V.** 55-20 wine. **W.** cordial.

tard cup; sugar; vase; cordial; large pitcher; punch bowl; and plate.

    55-1 12" console bowl, also made crimpt and sold as 55-1-1 in metal basket

    55-2 lily bowl (also sold as torte plate)

    55-3 6" covered compote

    55-4 8" open compote

    55-5 small cream/sugar set

    55-6 cup

    55-7 goblet

    55-8 4" covered jelly compote

    55-9 1 qt. water pitcher

    55-10 15" plate

    55-11 10" plate

    55-12 8" salad plate

    55-14 punch bowl and 55-14 15-piece punch set (consisted of 55-1 bowl, 55-10 15" plate, a dozen 55-6 cups and a ladle)

    55-15 9" salver

    55-16 4" round sauce

    55-17 saucer

    55-18 sherbet

    55-19 tumbler

    55-20 wine

NO. 56 PRISCILLA

Most of the moulds for this pattern were made for Wright in 1962-63 by Botson at B. Machine and Mould. The pattern was first on the market in 1963, and the line reached fourteen different items by 1966.

Wright may have been inspired by the Dalzell, Gilmore and Leighton Company's Alexis pattern, which was introduced in January, 1895. More likely, he was influenced by Fenton's Priscilla, a short-lived line made in the early 1950s.

56-1 4" covered compote
56-2 goblet
56-3 5" round sauce
56-4 toothpick
56-5 7" ash tray
56-6 6½" nappy
56-7 8" plate
56-8 rose bowl
56-9 sherbet
56-10 wine
56-11 6" covered compote
56-12 7" open compote
56-14 low bowl
56-15 4" low covered bowl

NO. 59 STIPPLE STAR

This pattern was first sold by Wright in 1959-60, and all of the moulds were made at Albert Botson's B. Machine and Mold in Cambridge, Ohio. In addition to these items, several Stipple Star lamp fonts and shades in several sizes were in Wright's lamp offerings over the years. Wright's inspiration was a nineteenth century McKee motif.

59-1 8" covered compote
59-2 6" covered compote
59-3 cream
59-4 covered sugar
59-5 salt dip
59-6 goblet
59-7 wine
59-8 fairy lamp w/candle

NO. 60 TREE OF LIFE

The items listed below began to appear in Wright listings during the mid-1960s, and all were made from moulds crafted by Albert Botson. The first Wright Master Catalog linked this pattern to the 1860s, but noted that the Wright firm had added its own design flourish, "eternal flame" stems and knobs.

60-1 deep crimp bowl, 6" d.
60-2 tall 4" covered compote
60-3 5" finger bowl
60-4 goblet

60-5 5½" crimpt nappy
60-6 4" three-toed round sauce
60-7 8" handled relish
60-8 footed wine
60-9 footed crimpt compote

NO. 64 THISTLE

This pattern began modestly in the late 1940s with the goblet and square plate (both moulds made by Weishar's Island Mould and Machine Co. in 1948), but it was greatly enlarged in the 1970s. The expansion began in 1969 when salesman W. C. (Red) Roetteis saw a Panelled Thistle butterdish during dinner at a relative's home in Kentucky. This pattern (called Delta) had originated with the J. B. Higbee Glass Company of Bridgeville, Pa., and was continued when some moulds were sold to the New Martinsville Glass Manufacturing Co. about 1918.

Red borrowed the butterdish from his aunt, Inez Metcalfe, and Si Wright soon became enthusiastic about developing this pattern line. Wright asked his sales force to search for old articles in Panelled Thistle, and these inspired many articles from moulds made by Botson after Wright's death. New items, some bearing a representation of the old Higbee trademark (a bee with the letters HIG on the wings and body), appeared regularly in the 1970s. Sales were excellent, and Thistle became the company's best selling crystal pattern. A few items were made in Ice Pink in 1990-91.

64-1 5½" bowl
64-2 7½" bowl
64-3 goblet
64-4 7½" square plate
64-5 8" oval relish
64-6 salt dip
64-7 wine
64-8 cream
64-9 sugar and cover
64-10 honey and cover
64-11 butter and cover
64-12 toothpick
64-14 salt and pepper shakers
64-15 sugar shaker
64-16 spooner
64-17 6" flared compote
64-18 6" covered compote
64-19 water pitcher
64-20 cruet

Stipple Star lamp.

64-21 round sauce
64-22 tall cream
64-23 tall open sugar
64-24 tumbler
64-25 low covered bowl
64-26 handled sauce
64-27 basket
64-28 nut tray
64-29 10" cake salver
64-30 7" salad plate
64-31 footed sauce
64-32 stemmed sherbet
64-33 fairy lamp
64-34 large basket

64-35 candleholder (made from handled
      sauce)
64-36 5" oval bowl
64-37 10" plate
64-38 large goblet
64-39 7½"" footed plate
64-40 10" footed plate
64-41 large sugar with cover
64-42 4" covered compote
64-43 cup
64-44 candleholder w/chimney, decorated

NO. 65 THREE FACE

Wright's goblet and sherbet (also called sauce) were both on the market in the 1930s, and the compote moulds were made by Weishar's Island Mould and Machine Co. in 1947. Weishar made the salt/pepper shaker mould in 1950.

The four new pieces added in 1971 (cream; sugar and cover; sugar shaker; and spooner) resulted after salesman Red Roetteis purchased an old Three Face cream and covered sugar and sent them to Wright. Botson started on the moulds in 1969 before Si Wright's death, and Mrs. Wright had the work completed and introduced the pieces.

65-1 6" covered compote
65-2 4" covered compote
65-3 goblet
65-4 lamp base
65-5 lamp base w/burner and chimney
65-6 salt dip
65-7 salt and pepper shakers
65-8 sherbet
65-9 toothpick
65-10 wine or claret
65-11 cream
65-12 sugar and cover
65-14 sugar shaker
65-15 spooner

NO. 66 WESTWARD HO

Obviously seeking to capitalize on the great popularity of a nineteenth century motif, Wright first marketed the goblet, sherbet and wine, probably in the late 1930s. In March, 1940, Lee illustrated an interesting small lamp made from the goblet, an idea typical of Wright's thinking.

The 6" compote moulds were made by Weishar's Island Mould and Machine Co. in 1946. Botson made several moulds (cream; covered

Three Face from 1972-73 Wright catalog.

Westward Ho from 1972-73 Wright catalog.

sugar; and celery vase) in the late 1960s.

66-1 6" oval covered compote
66-2 6" round covered compote
66-3 goblet
66-4 sherbet
66-5 wine
66-6 5" round covered compote
66-6 5" low round covered compote
66-7 4" covered compote (made from sherbet
    and sugar lid)
66-8 covered butter
66-9 cream
66-10 covered sugar
66-11 celery vase
66-12 tumbler

NO. 67 WILDFLOWER

Wildflower square plates can be found in the Wright inventories during the 1940s in crystal, amber, blue and green, and the goblets likely appeared during the same decade. The Wildflower line was greatly expanded when Botson completed a number of moulds in 1959-1960, and a dozen different articles were available throughout the 1960s.

67-1 6" covered compote (Botson mould 1959)
67-2 4" covered compote (Botson mould 1959)
67-3 cream (Botson mould 1959)
67-4 covered sugar (Botson mould 1960)
67-5 goblet
67-6 9½" square plate
67-7 rectangular salt dip
67-8 crescent salt dip (Botson mould1960)
67-9 footed sauce dish
67-10 covered stick candy jar
67-11 7½" footed vase (Botson mould 1959)
67-12 wine

NO. 70 COVERED CANDY BOXES

This category is based upon function rather than pattern, so it includes quite a few Wright items which also appear elsewhere in the line. The Atterbury Duck moulds were made by Weishar's Island Mould and Machine Co. in 1941, and this same firm made the 7" Hen on Nest moulds in 1947. The Acorn Squirrel covered candy box, which was discontinued before 1962, was likely made from Weishar-made moulds, too. Botson made the moulds for the 3" Hen as well as the Stove, the Violin and several others.

70-1 Cabbage Leaf
70-2 Atterbury Duck
70-3 Embossed Rose 6" four-toed
70-4 Fish
70-5 Flat Iron
70-6 Frog
70-7 3" Hen
70-8 7" Hen on Nest
70-9 Horse Shoe
70-10 9" Rabbit Atterbury-type
70-11 Stove
70-12 large Turtle
70-14 Violin
70-15 Embossed Rose 4" 4-toed
70-16 tall Wildrose covered compote
70-17 large Turkey
70-18 3" Hen

NO. 72 OPEN COMPOTES

Just a few items are included here, and many overlap with other segments of the Wright line, especially since they are made from goblets. The 72-3 Dolphin compote, however, is one of the most significant pieces of Wright glass; this is an original Northwood mould (c. 1897) which was acquired by Wright in 1939 and immediately used to make glass.

72-1 Daisy and Cube
72-2 Daisy and Cube with Forest deep plate
    etching
72-3 Dolphin compote
72-4 large Maple Leaf compote
72-5 Strawberry and Currant
72-6 Wildrose open compote
72-7 large Wildrose open compote

NO. 75 VASES AND ROSE BOWLS

Several interesting items are in this category. The well-known 75-1 Corn vase was first made by the Dugan Glass Co. in Indiana, Pa., about 1905. This vase was one of the old moulds bought by Wright in 1939, and it appeared in the Wright line in blue opalescent and vaseline opalescent within just a few months. It was in the line for decades, eventually being renumbered as 77-121 in Wright's 1978 Catalog Supplement The 75-3 Petticoat vase is also an old Northwood mould (see *Harry Northwood: The Early Years*, p. 116).

75-1 Corn vase
75-2 Embossed Rose 8" vase
75-3 6" Petticoat vase

75-4 Embossed Rose rose bowl
75-5 7" Maize pattern rose bowl
75-5 10" vase crimpt top (w/thumbprint)
75-6 10" vase crimpt top (mint green overlay satin)
75-7 10" vase crimpt top (amber overlay satin)

NO. 76 CARDINAL

In the early 1960s, salesman Red Roetteis sent an old Cardinal goblet and a creamer to L. G. Wright, and Wright decided to have moulds made. He planned to decorate the bird with red (as a cardinal) or blue (as a blue jay) and to expand the line by adding other pieces. As it turned out, these moulds did not work well, and relatively small quantities of the Cardinal goblets (76-1) were made.

NO. 77 MISCELLANEOUS

With over 130 separate items, this is by far the most lengthy area of the L. G. Wright line. Some articles are individual novelties or single items (especially goblets) in a given pattern that reflects a Victorian-ear motif. Sometimes there are several pieces (or a group of items) in a particular pattern, but the articles are separated and found in different places in the 77 classification; among these are the patterns Daisy and Cube, Sweetheart, S, Embossed Rose, Diamond Quilted, Sawtooth, Strawberry and Currant, Morning Glory, Princess Feather, Mirror and Rose, Magnet and Grape, and Grape.

On other occasions, an item or two in the 77-series, such as the Baltimore Pear Goblet or the Cabbage Leaf goblet and wine, were the only articles in the line after the early 1960s. Some Wright items discontinued prior to 1962 (Berry goblet; Kings Crown goblet, crystal or ruby-stained; Pineapple goblet; Baltimore Pear goblet, Broken Column goblet, Deer and Pine Tree goblet; Shell and Tassel goblet and Frosted Ribbon goblet) were reintroduced later.

The S pattern pieces were based upon an old motif called Erie, which was first made at Indiana, Pa., in 1903. Wright may have acquired some moulds in his 1939 purchase. The pattern, called "S-Repeat" by glass collectors, is popular, and Wright had Botson make several moulds for articles that were never part of the original Erie line. Likewise, Wright's Sweetheart items were based upon a c. 1905 Dugan pattern originally called

Victor (popularly known today as Jewelled Heart).

77-1 Colonial Carriage ash tray
77-2 Fish ash tray or spoon tray
77-3 Leaf ash tray
77-4 Panel Daisy ash tray
77-5 Ram's head ash tray
77-6 Violin ash tray
77-7 Chick covered basket
77-8 Bee Hive
77-9 Three-Wheel Cart
77-10 Daisy and Cube cream and sugar
77-11 Sweetheart cream and sugar (also used for sugar and cover alone)
77-12 S cruet
77-14 Grape decanter
77-15 miniature dust pan (inspired by a turn of-the-century product of the Indiana Tumbler and Goblet Co., this mould was made by Botson in 1958)
77-16 Embossed Rose Triangle fairy lamp
77-17 Acorn goblet
77-18 Artichoke goblet
77-19 Cabbage Leaf goblet
77-20 Cable goblet
77-21 Daisy and Cube goblet
77-22 Daisy and Cube goblet with Forest deep plate etching
77-23 Diamond Quilted goblet
77-24 Grasshopper goblet
77-25 Herringbone goblet (mould made by Weishar's Island Mould and Machine Co. in 1948)
77-26 Horn of Plenty goblet
77-27 Inverted Dot goblet
77-28 Lion frosted goblet
77-29 Maple Leaf goblet
77-30 Morning Glory goblet
77-31 Panel Daisy goblet
77-32 Plume goblet
77-33 Princess Feather goblet (Botson mould 1962)
77-34 S goblet
77-35 Sawtooth goblet (Botson mould 1960)
77-36 Strawberry and Currant goblet
77-37 Sweetheart goblet
77-38 Thistle goblet
77-39 Two Panel goblet
77-40 Wheat and Barley goblet (Botson mould 1962)
77-41 Wildrose 12 oz. goblet

CHAPTER SIX

77-42 101 Ranch goblet

77-43 Thousand Eye goblet

77-44 mayonnaise ladle

77-45 Strawberry and Currant mug (Botson mould 1959)

77-46 Ferdinand mustard jar

77-47 Embossed Rose Triangle nappy

77-48 Crescent planter

77-49 Lion bread plate

77-50 Bird salt dip

77-51 Frog salt dip (Botson mould 1960)

77-52 Swan salt dip

77-53 Thistle salt dip

77-54 Embossed Rose salt and pepper shakers

77-55 Fluted Vine salt and pepper shakers

77-56 stopper for cruets

77-57 Princess Feather tulip sundae (made from goblet)

77-58 Basket toothpick (two-handled), with chick (Botson mould 1956)

77-59 Fish toothpick

77-60 Frog toothpick

77-61 Rabbit toothpick (Botson mould 1960)

77-62 Rooster toothpick (Botson mould 1960)

77-63 S toothpick

77-64 Sweetheart toothpick

77-65 Tree Stump toothpick

77-66 Diamond Quilted wine

77-67 Morning Glory wine

77-68 Strawberry and Currant wine (Botson —mould 1959)

77-69 Wildrose 5 oz. wine (Botson mould 1962)

77-70 Cabbage Leaf wine

77-71 S wine

77-72 Coal Hod ash tray with wire bail (Botson mould 1963)

77-73 Wildrose 12 oz. iced tea (Botson mould 1963)

77-74 S plate

77-75 Hoot Owl relish (Botson mould 1963)

77-76 S sherbet

77-77 Panel Sawtooth wine (Botson mould 1963)

77-78 Wildrose 8" 3-toed footed nappy

77-79 Mirror and Rose goblet (Botson mould 1964-65)

77-80 Panel Sawtooth sherbet (Botson mould 1964)

77-81 Daisy and Cube wine; also made as 77 81-10, decorated with "Flower Band" (Botson mould 1964)

77-82 Sweetheart wine

77-83 Magnet and Grape goblet

77-84 Magnet and Grape wine

77-85 Mirror and Rose wine

77-86 Wildrose 7" ash tray

77-87 Wildrose 6" ash tray

77-88 Wildrose 4" ash tray

77-89 Wildrose 3-pc. ash tray set

77-90 Grape pattern large oval bowl, four toed (Botson mould 1964-65)

77-91 Hi Button Shoe [Mosser mould; glass bought by Wright]

77-92 Queen Anne Slipper [Mosser mould; glass bought by Wright]

77-93 Turkey toothpick [Mosser mould; glass bought by Wright]

77-94 Strawberry and Currant creamer

77-95 Pump

77-96 Trough

77-97 large 16 oz. Wildrose goblet (Botson mould 1962)

77-98 Ribbed Palm Leaf goblet (Botson mould 1962)

77-99 Sawtooth ice tea (Botson mould 1967)

77-100 Sawtooth toothpick

77-101 Wildrose butter and cover

77-102 Broken Column goblet

77-103 Deer & Pine Tree goblet

77-104 Frosted Ribbon goblet

77-105 Rose Sprig goblet

77-106 Shell and Tassel goblet (a Shell and Tassel oval footed compote mould was made by Weishar's Island Mould and Machine Co. in 1949)

77-107 Mirror and Rose salt and pepper shakers (Botson mould 1968)

77-108 Mirror and Rose pickle jar w/metal cover

77-109 Butterfly ash tray(Botson mould 1968)

77-110 S cup

77-111 6" Grape bowl (also 77-111C w/candlewell); also called Grape and Cable oval bowl (Botson mould 1969)

77-112 Baltimore Pear goblet

77-114 Stork goblet

77-115 Sweetheart fairy lamp w/candle (add A for amber, B blue, G green and R ruby)

77-120 Sweetheart oil lamps (these may have colored fonts—opal, ruby or amber, or they may be decorated opal— Buttercup, Strawberry, Violet or Floral)

77-121 Corn vase (see 75-1 above)
77-122 oil lamp Kings Crown base, Daisy and Button font
77-123 oil lamp Kings Crown base, Beaded font
77-124 oil lamp (burner attached to syrup pitcher)
77-125 Grape rose bowl
77-126 Grape nut bowl
77-127 Frog candy with cover
77-128 9" Rabbit with cover
77-129 Chicken on Basket toothpick
77-130 tee pee cruet
77-131 small paperweight
77-132 large paperweight
77-133 small bird

NO. 78 STORK AND RUSHES

Except for the sugar bowl cover, all of these were made from the original Dugan moulds, which were among the group purchased by Wright in 1939. They were shown in Carnival (amethyst Carnival glass), crystal satin, Marigold (marigold Carnival glass), and pale blue milk glass in Wright's 1975 Catalog Supplement.

78-1 water pitcher
78-2 berry bowl
78-3 spooner
78-4 covered sugar
78-5 cream
78-7 sauce

NO. 80 ANIMAL CANDY BOXES

Most collectors call these attractive animal items "covered dishes" today, and they are quite popular. Most of Wright's were inspired by McKee pieces which date back to the last quarter of the nineteenth century.

80-1 5" Bird
80-2 5" Cat
80-3 5" Cow (Botson mould 1961)
80-4 5" Dog
80-5 5" Duck (Botson mould 1961)
80-6 5" Frog
80-7 5" Hen
80-8 5" Horse
80-9 5" Lamb
80-10 5" Owl
80-11 5" Rabbit
80-12 5" Rooster

80-14 5" Swan
80-15 5" Turkey
80-16 5" Turtle

NOS. 84-98 BLOWN WARE

In classifications 84- through 98- (all of which are blown items), the number which follows the hyphen designates a particular motif imparted by the initial spot mould: -1 is thumbprint; -2 is fern; -3 is dot; -4 is swirl; -5 is honeycomb; -6 is eye dot, etc. The system tends to break down after -10, however, for decorated pieces made in overlay glass sometimes appear where one expects a spot mould motif. One must also realize that not every item was made with all the possible spot mould motifs.

Over the years, Wright's most popular color was certainly "cranberry," and the firm generally did not differentiate between cranberry and cranberry opalescent (almost all of the cranberry pieces are shown in Wright's 1973 Master Catalog). Some items were also made in amethyst and blue opalescent during the 1940s-1950s, and vaseline and vaseline opalescent were popular for many years. Blue opalescent made a comeback in the late 1970s, and some items were made in cobalt blue opalescent, too.

NO. 84 WATER PITCHERS

84-1 thumbprint
84-2 fern
84-3 dot
84-4 swirl
84-5 honeycomb

NO. 85 MILK PITCHERS

85-1 milk pitcher w/thumbprint
85-2 milk pitcher w/fern
85-4 milk pitcher w/swirl
85-5 milk pitcher w/honeycomb
85-7 milk pitcher, diamond quilted
84-9 milk pitcher w/rib
85-11 milk pitcher w/swirl

NOS. 86-87 APOTHECARY JARS

86-1 medium oval, thumbprint
86-2 medium oval
87-1 large oval, thumbprint
87-2 large oval

NOS. 88-89 BARBER BOTTLES

89-1 round barber bottle w/thumbprint
88-2 fluted barber bottle w/fern
88-4 fluted barber bottle w/swirl
88-6 fluted barber bottle w/eye dot
88-10 fluted barber bottle w/rib
89-11 barber bottle RO (may be decorated)

NO. 90 CREAM PITCHERS

90-1 tall cream w/thumbprint
90-2 tall cream w/fern
90-3 tall cream w/dot
90-4 tall cream w/swirl
90-5 tall cream w/honeycomb
90-6 tall cream w/eye dot
90-7 tall cream, quilted
90-8 tall cream, stars and stripes
90-11 tall cream w/swirl
90-12 tall cream, quilted
90-40 tall cream Peach Blow, decorated
    Moss Rose

NO. 91 CREAM AND SUGAR SET

91-1 short cream and sugar w/thumbprint

NOS. 92-95 CRUETS

92-1 fluted cruet w/thumbprint
92-6 fluted cruet w/eye dot
93-1 fluted vine cruet w/thumbprint
93-7 fluted vine cruet, quilted
94-1 oval cruet w/thumbprint
94-2 oval cruet w/fern
94-3 oval cruet w/dot
94-4 oval cruet w/swirl
94-5 oval cruet w/honeycomb
95-1 round cruet w/thumbprint
95-2 round cruet w/fern
95-3 round cruet w/dot
95-4 round cruet w/swirl
95-11 round cruet w/swirl
95-40 round cruet Peach Blow, decorated
    Moss Rose

NO. 96 SUGAR SHAKERS
AND SYRUP PITCHERS

96-1 sugar shaker w/thumbprint
96-2 sugar shaker w/fern
96-3 sugar shaker w/dot
96-4 sugar shaker w/swirl
96A-2 syrup pitcher w/fern
96A-4 syrup pitcher w/swirl
96A-5 syrup pitcher w/honeycomb
96-11 sugar shaker w/swirl

NO. 97 TUMBLERS

97-1 tumbler w/thumbprint
97-2 tumbler w/fern
97-3 tumbler w/dot
97-4 tumbler w/swirl
97-5 tumbler w/honeycomb
97-6 tumbler w/eye dot
97-8 tumbler w/stars and stripes

NO. 98 PICKLE JARS

98-1-5 pickle jar w/thumbprint
98-2-5 pickle jar w/fern
98-3-5 pickle jar w/dot
98-4-5 pickle jar w/swirl
22-36-5 Daisy and Button pickle jar
40-8-5 Maize pickle jar
99-40-5 Peach Blow, decorated Moss Rose
(note: other numerical designations were used for pickle jars in various frames, including a fancy one with four toes).

NO. 99 DECORATED ITEMS

Most of these articles are opal (milk) glass, and the Wright firm established a strong reputation for decorated ware in this color. In the 1940s and 1950s, Wright used small decorating firms such as the Zarilla Art Glass Co. Later, milk glass was made and decorated with Wright's designs at Davis-Lynch in Star City, West Virginia. Some articles were also made in amber or green and decorated with the Daisy or Rose designs. Wright's favorite design, and perhaps the most long-lived, was surely Moss Rose.

After the firm set up its own decorating department in 1968, many new designs were developed, and this effort continues at Wright Glass today. Although every decoration was not available on each different article, the names of just a few of Wright's decorations reflect many different floral motifs: Daisy, Grey Rose, Holland Rose, Pansy, Rose [sometimes called Red Rose], Spring Bouquet, Wildrose. As the number of decorations grew larger, the Wright firm assigned different digits after the hyphen to differentiate the articles in its price listings. For example, the round candy box appears as 99-25 in amber (Daisy decoration) and as 99-26 (Rose decoration).

The following listing, by no means all-inclusive, offers insight into the vast array of Wright's decorated ware.

99-6 14" slim vase
99-9 round candy box and cover
99-14 8" round vase
99-15 9" picture vase (mould made by Weishar's Island Mould and Machine Co. in 1950)
99-16 8" convex vase
99-18 large oval apothecary jar
99-19 13" ball shape vase (cf. 99-30)
99-20 13" pear shape vase
99-21 6" apothecary jar
99-22 8" apothecary jar
99-23 10" apothecary jar
99-24 12" apothecary jar
99-30 13" ball shape vase dec. Holland Rose
99-31 round candy box and cover decorated Holland Rose
99-32 13" ball shape vase amber optic decorated Rose
99-33 13" ball shape vase amber optic dec. Daisy
99-34 13" ball shape vase green optic dec. Rose
99-35 13" ball shape vase green optic decorated Daisy
99-36 round candy box and cover green optic decorated Rose
99-37 round candy box and cover green optic decorated Daisy
99-38 6" apothecary jar decorated Blue Holland Rose
99-39 8" apothecary jar decorated Blue Holland Rose
99-40 10" apothecary jar decorated Blue Holland Rose

Text continued on page 161.

Decorated apothecary jars in various sizes.

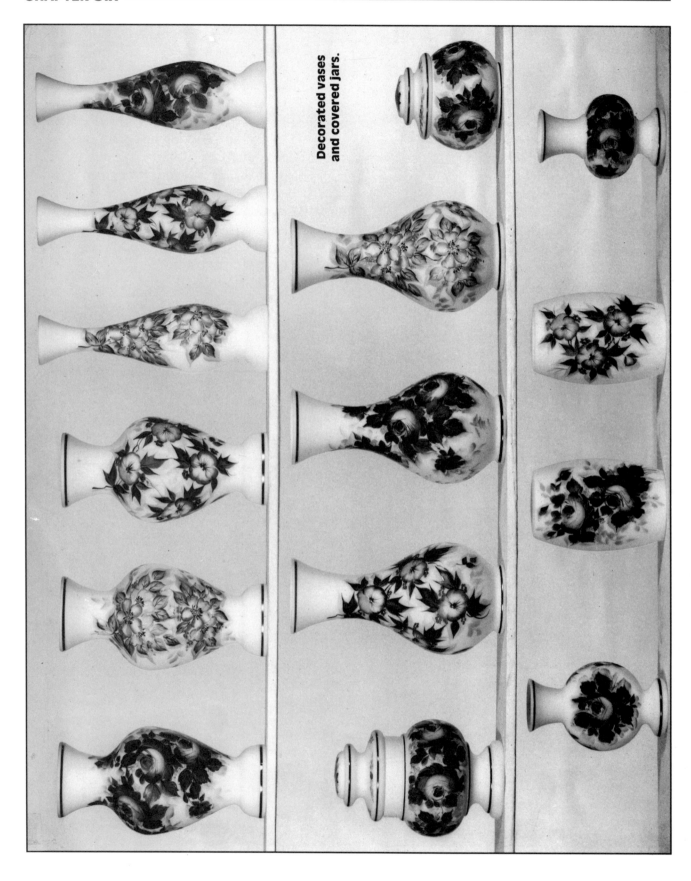

Decorated vases and covered jars.

Decorated Wedding bowls.

In the course of preparing this book, the authors were allowed complete access to the L. G. Wright Glass Company's gift shop as well as the old sample room and storage areas which contained items discontinued from the Wright line long ago. In this eighty-page color section, more than one-third of the pages consist of glassware selected especially for this book or taken from original transparencies used for an L. G. Wright Master Catalog.

Other pages were selected from the portfolios of color photographs which were used by Wright's sales force in the 1960s, the era of the company's largest line and greatest sales. These photographs, taken by brothers James and Paul Pappas of Parkersburg, depict a wide variety of items from the Wright line, and articles were often arranged to show all the colors being offered at a particular time. Items shown on the color pages are numbered consecutively, and captions keyed to these numbers can be found on pages 173-187 of this book.

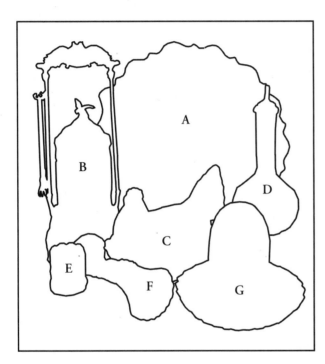

FRONT COVER

A. purple Carnival Peacock plate.

B. cobalt blue 77-108 Mirror and Rose pickle jar (white floral decoration).

C. vaseline opalescent 70-8 7" Hen on Nest.

D. Cranberry fluted barber bottle, fern.

E. amberina 7-8 cherry toothpick.

F. green Hand vase.

G. Peach Blow fairy light, decorated Moss Rose.

BACK COVER

H. Three Face lamp.

I. purple Carnival Grape decanter.

J. cranberry toy lamp, half shade, swirl.

K. green overlay Beaded Curtain cream (satin finish).

L. purple Carnival Grape wine.

M. amberina satin Grape 5" oval bowl.

N. cobalt blue 64-9 Thistle small sugar w/cover.

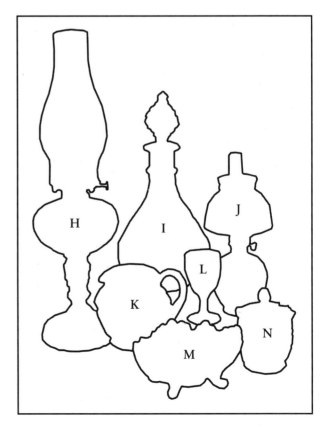

1 2 3 4

5 6 7 8 9

10 11 12 13

14 15 16 17

18　　19　　20　　21　　22　　23　　24

25　　26　　27　　28　　29　　30　　31

32　　33　　34　　35　　36

37　　38　　39　　40　　41　　42

82

43 44 45 46 47

48 49 50 51 52

53 54 55 56 57 58

59 60 61 62

83

63

64

65

66

67

68

69

70

71

72

73

74

75

76

77

78

79

84

80   81   82   83   84

85   86   87   88   89

90   91   92   93   94   95   96

97   98   99   100   101   102   103   104

140

141

142

143

144

145

146

147

148

149

150

151

152

153

154

155

156

157

158

159

160

161

162

163

164

165

166

167

168

169

170

171

172

174

176

175

173

177

91

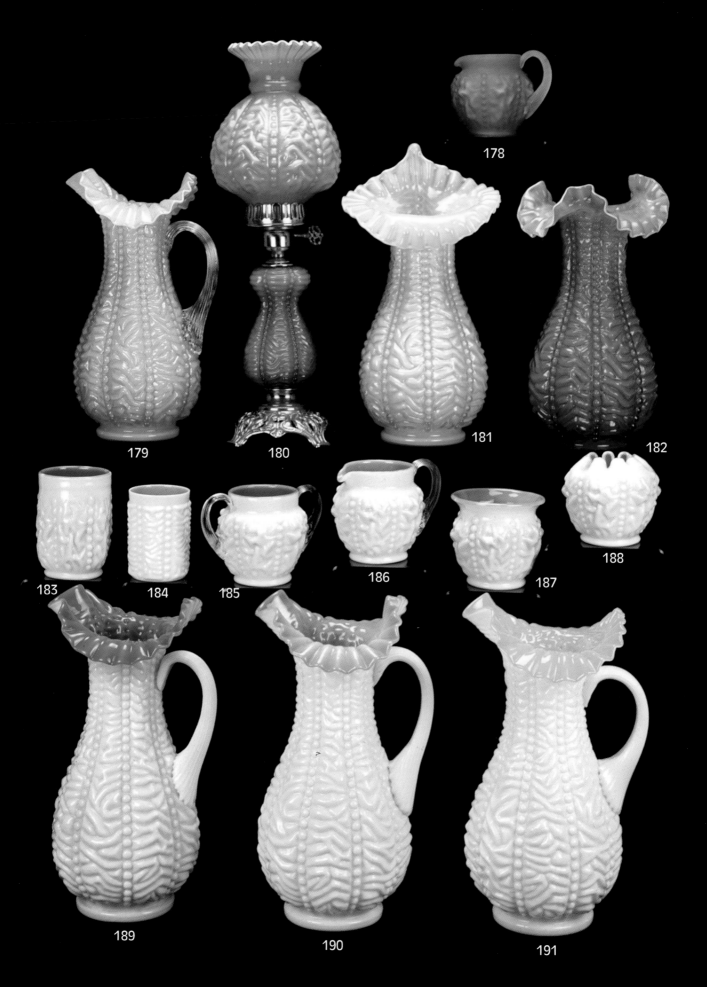

178

179   180   181   182

183   184   185   186   187   188

189   190   191

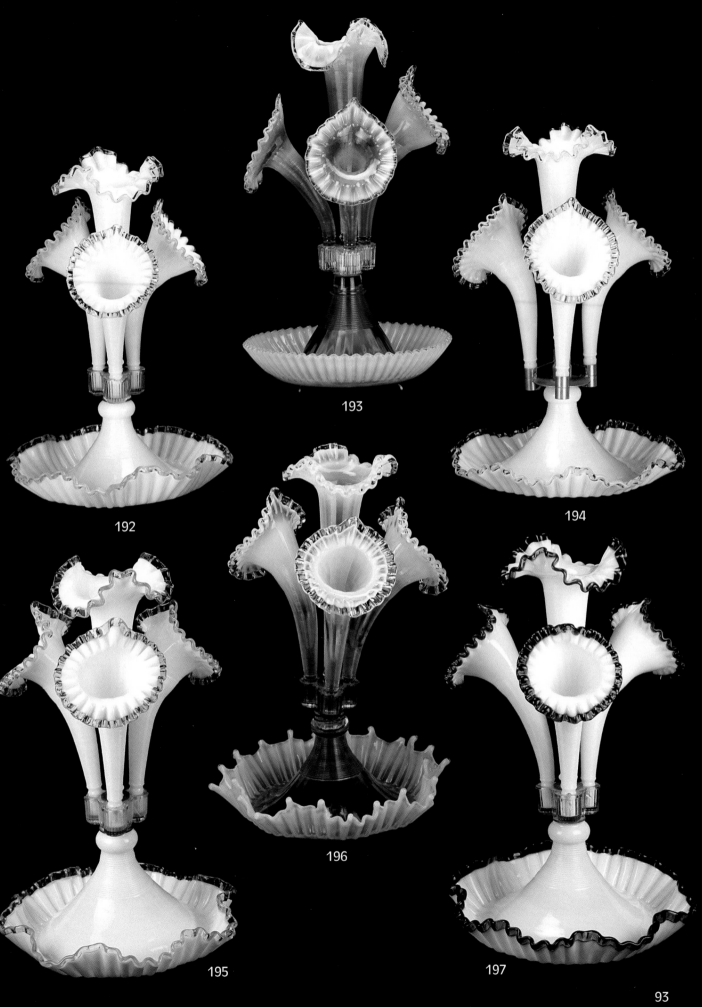

192

193

194

195

196

197

93

198

199

200

201 202 203 204 205

206 207 208 209 210

211 212

215 213

214 216

94

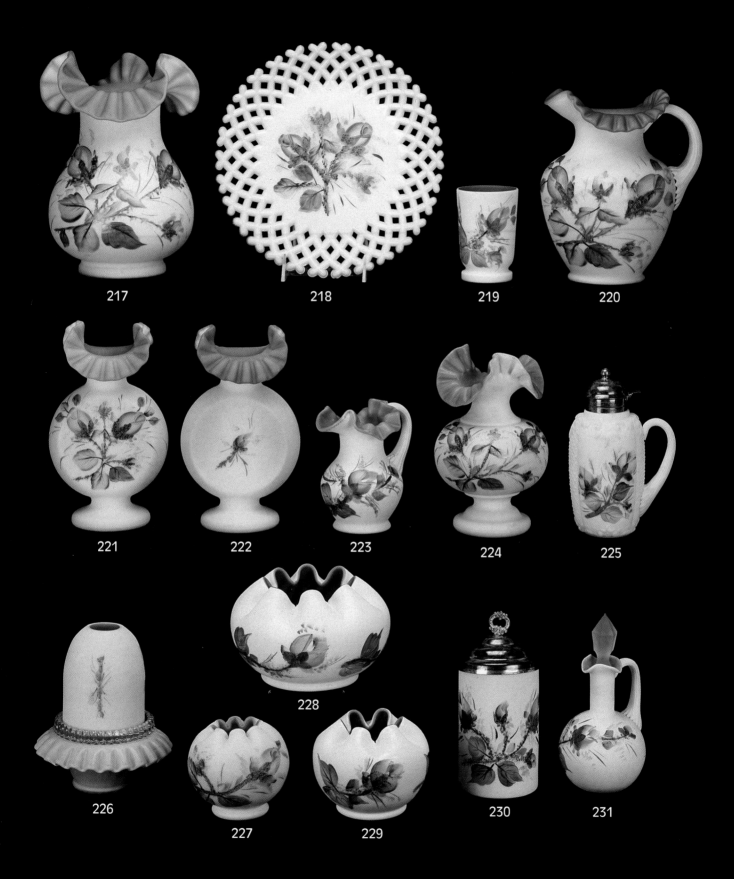

217

218

219

220

221

222

223

224

225

226

227

228

229

230

231

232

233

234

235

237

238

239

240

241

242

243

244

245

246 247 248 249 250 251 252

253 254 255 256

257 258 259

260   261   262   263

264   265   266   267

                269   271   273
268   270

                                        272

274

275

276

277

278

279

280

281

282

283

284

285

286

287

288

289

290

291

100

292

293

294

295

296

297

298

299

300

301

302

303

304

305

306

307

308

309

310

311

312

313

314

315

316

317

318

319

320

321

322

323

324

325

326

327

328

329

330

331

332

333

334

335

336

337

338

339

340

341

342

343

344

345

346

347

348

103

349

350

351

352

353

354

355

356

357

358

359

360

361

362

363

364

365

366

367   368   369   370   371

372   373   374   375   376   377

378   379   380

381   382   383   384   385

386

387

388

389

390

391

392

393

394

395

396

397

398

399

106

400

401

402

403

404

405

406

407   408   409   410 411

412 413 414 415 416 417 418

419 420   421   422   423

424   426   430

425   427 428 429

431

432 433

434

435 436 437 438 439 440 441

442 443 444 445

108 446 447 448 449 450

451

452

454

455

454

453

456

457

456

501 502 503 504 505

506 507 508 509 510 511

512 513 514 515 516

112 517 518 519 520 521

522 523 524 525 526 527

528 529 530 531 532 533 534

535 536 537 538 539

540 541 542 543

113

544

545

546

547

548

549

550

551

552

553

554

555

114

556

557

558

559

560

561

562

563

564

565

566

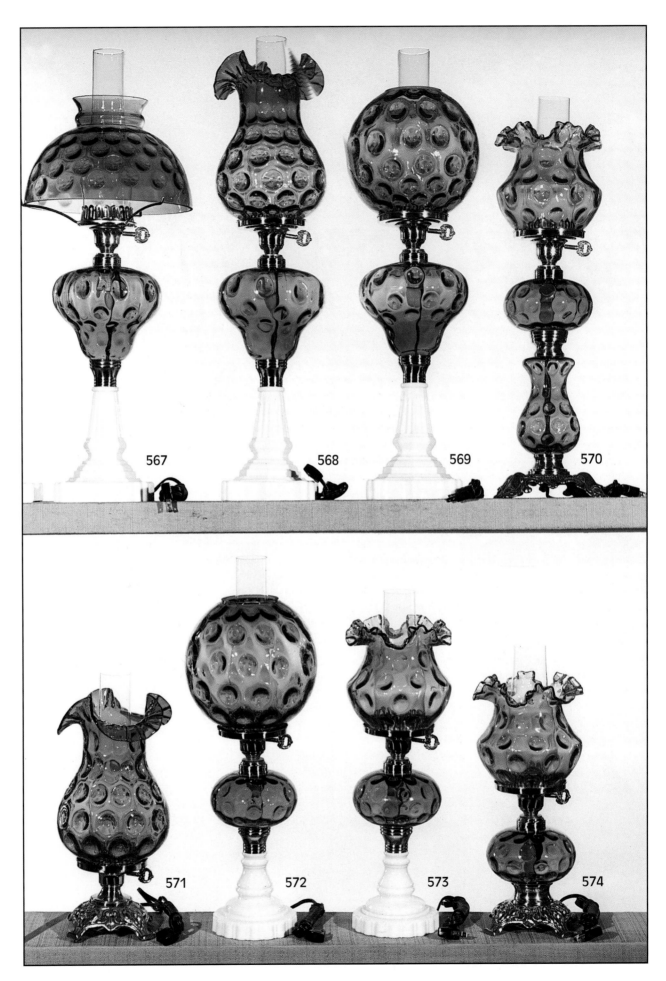

567   568   569   570

571   572   573   574

575   576   577   578

579   580   581   582

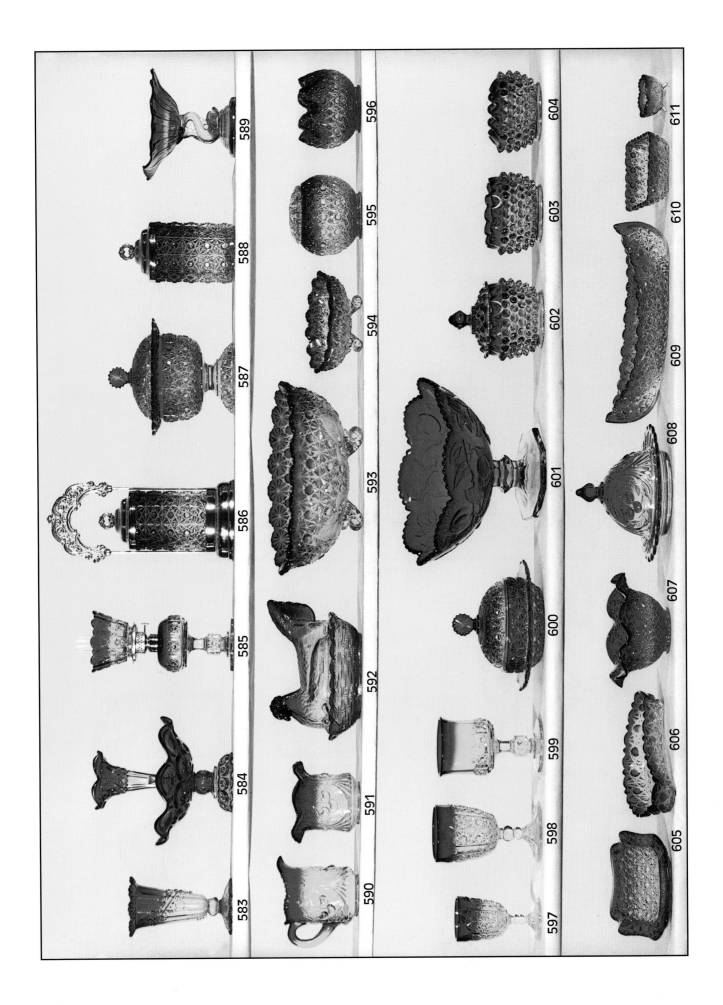

583 584 585 586 587 588 589

590 591 592 593 594 595 596

597 598 599 600 601 602 603 604

605 606 607 608 609 610 611

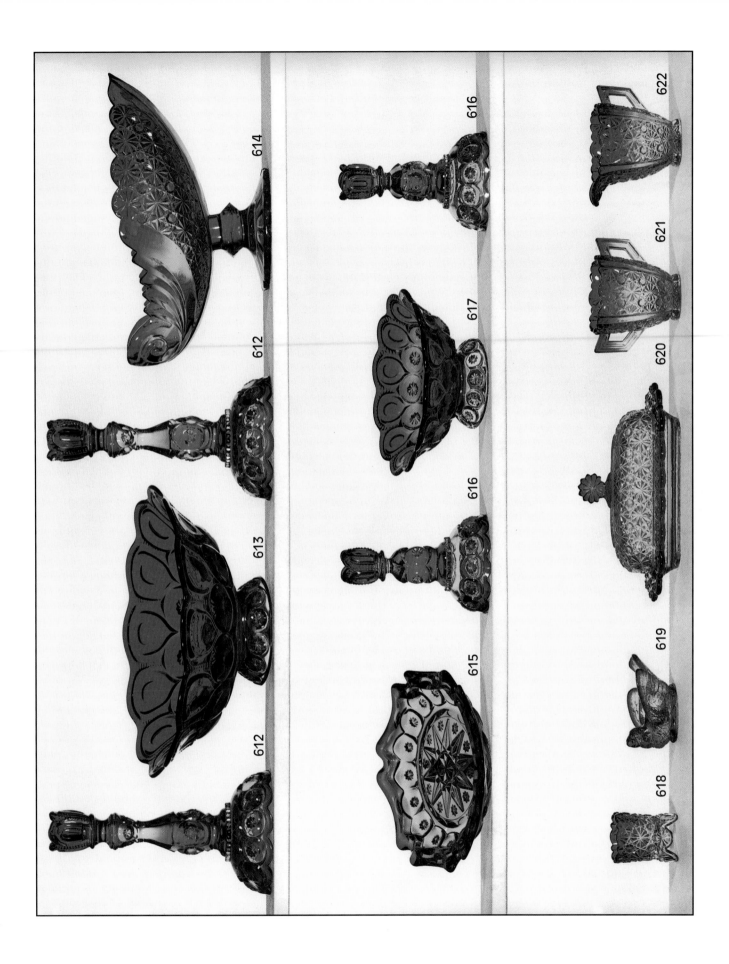

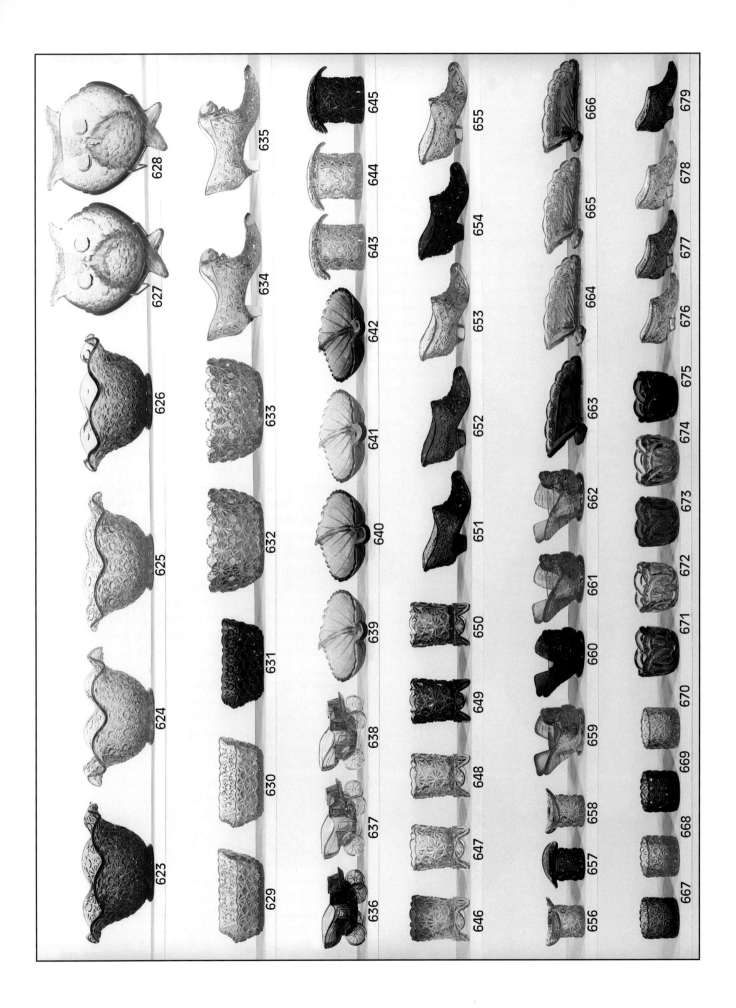

623 624 625 626 627 628

629 630 631 632 633 634 635

636 637 638 639 640 641 642 643 644 645

646 647 648 649 650 651 652 653 654 655

656 657 658 659 660 661 662 663 664 665 666

667 668 669 670 671 672 673 674 675 676 677 678 679

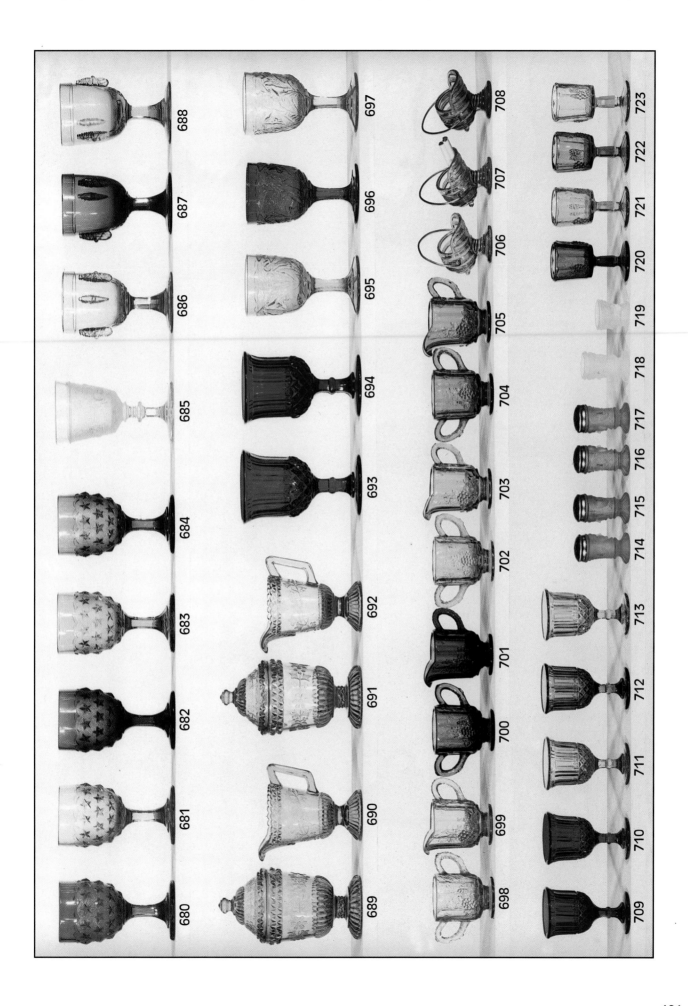

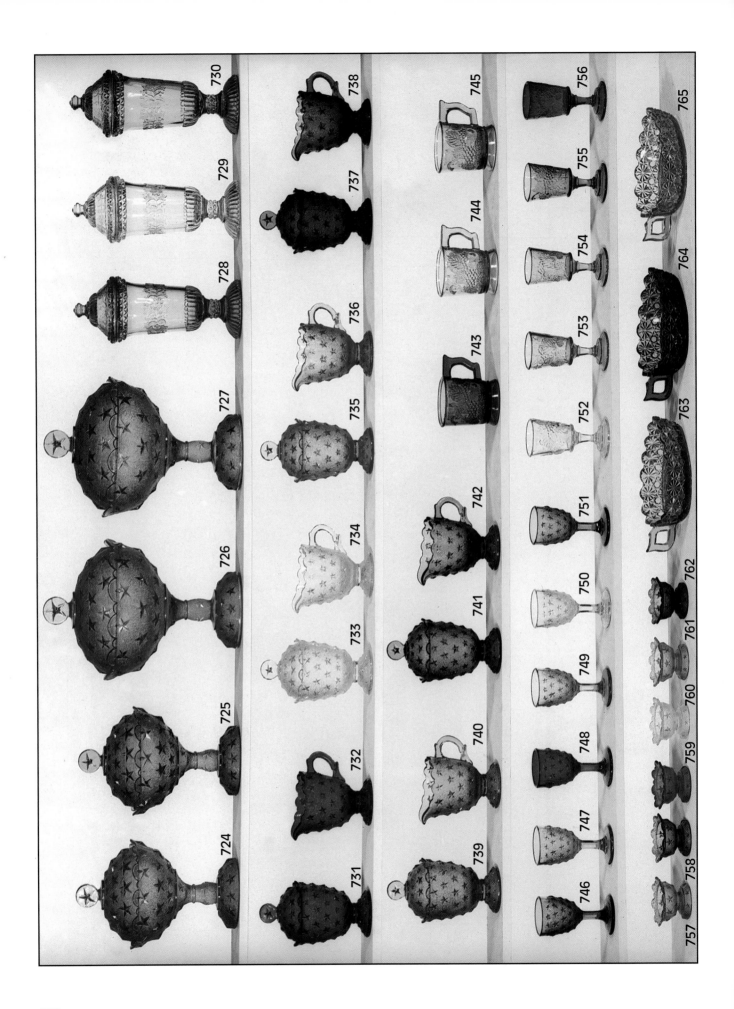

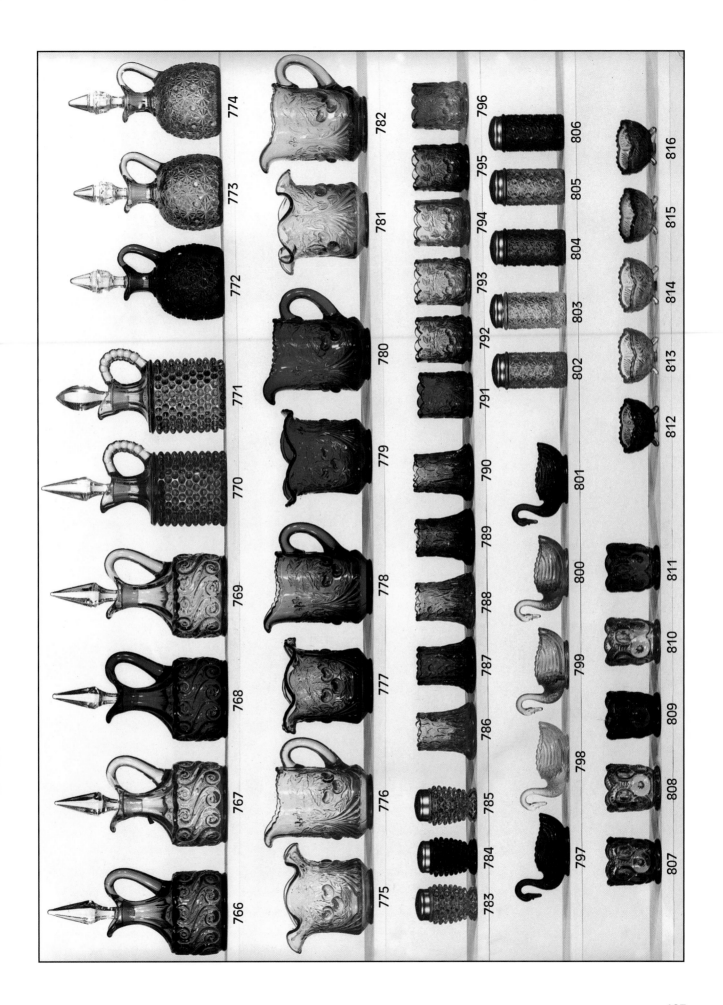

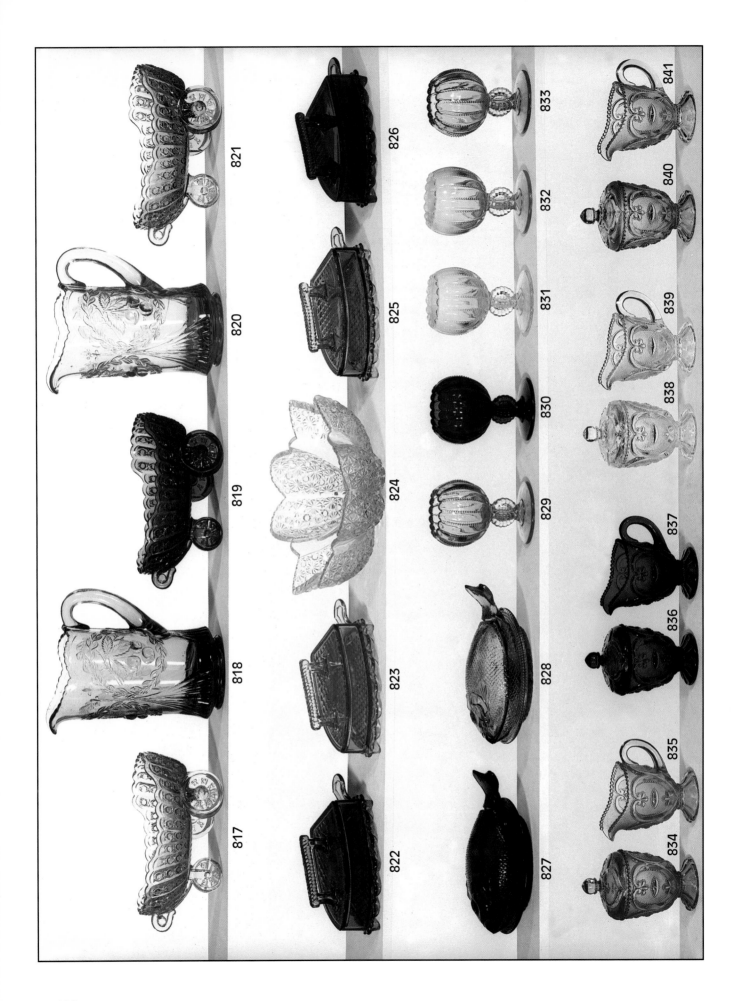

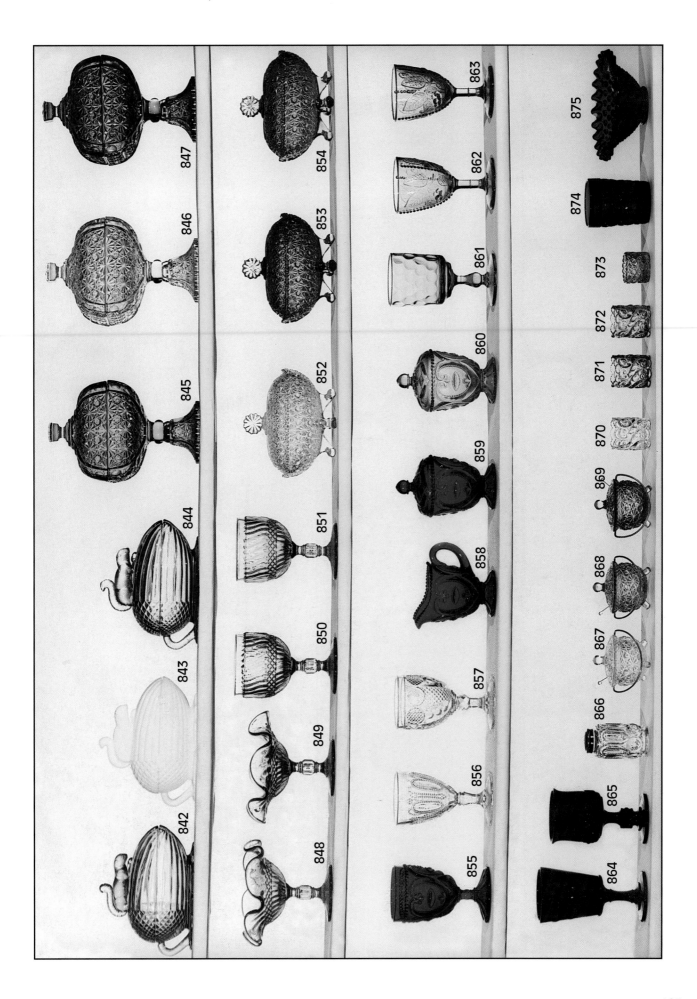

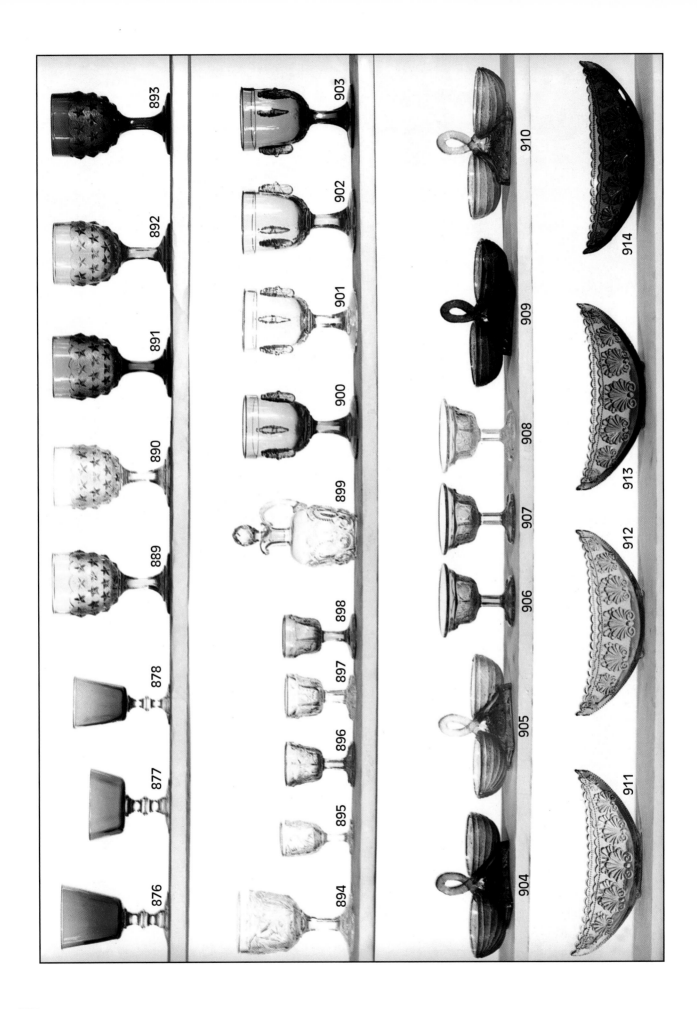

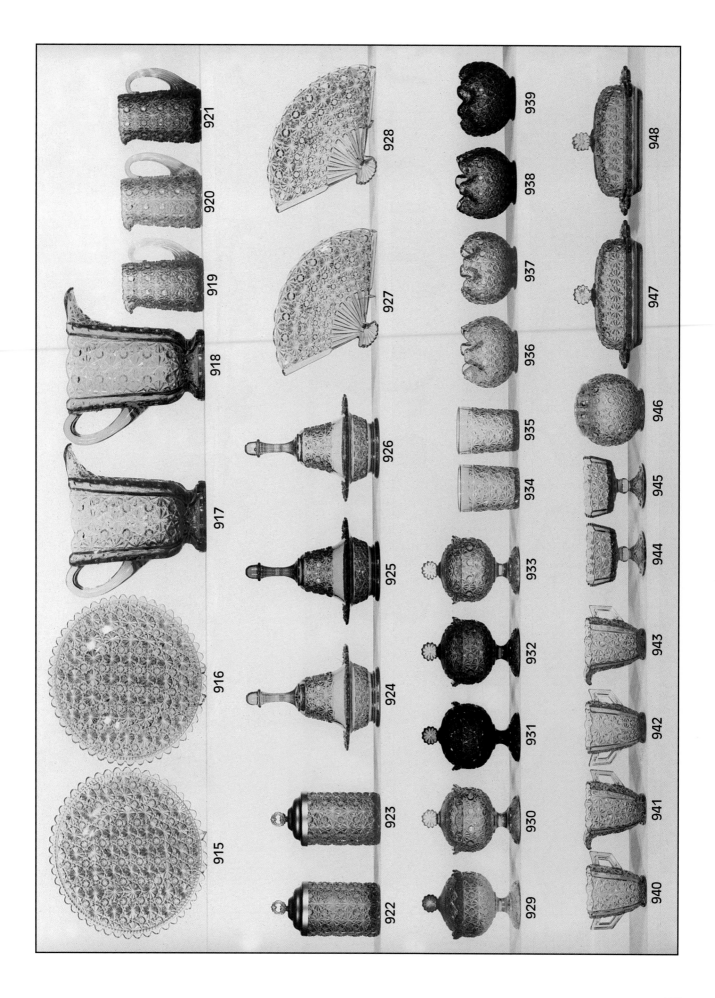

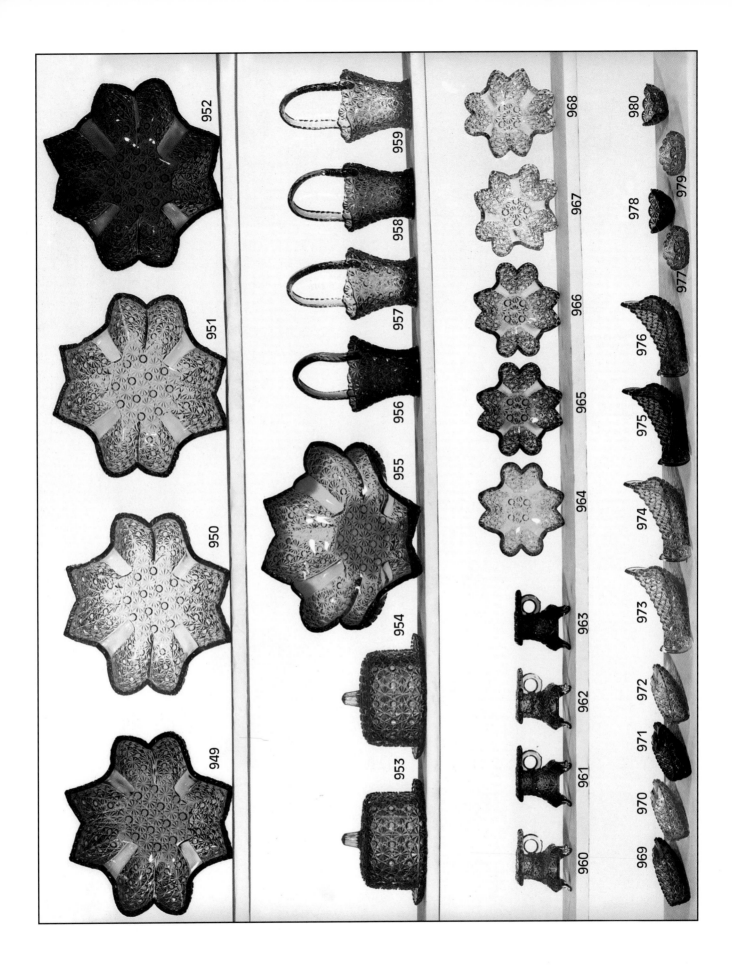

949 950 951 952

953 954 955 956 957 958 959

960 961 962 963 964 965 966 967 968

969 970 971 972 973 974 975 976 977 978 979 980

1033

1039

1045

1051

1032

1038

1044

1050

1031

1037

1043

1049

1030

1036

1042

1048

1029

1035

1041

1047

1028

1034

1040

1046

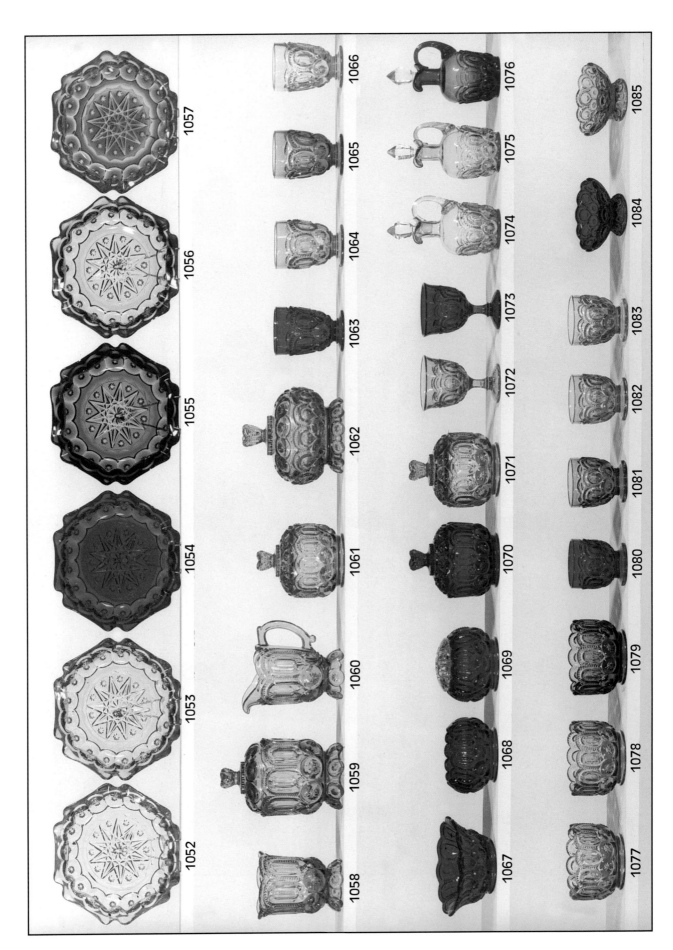

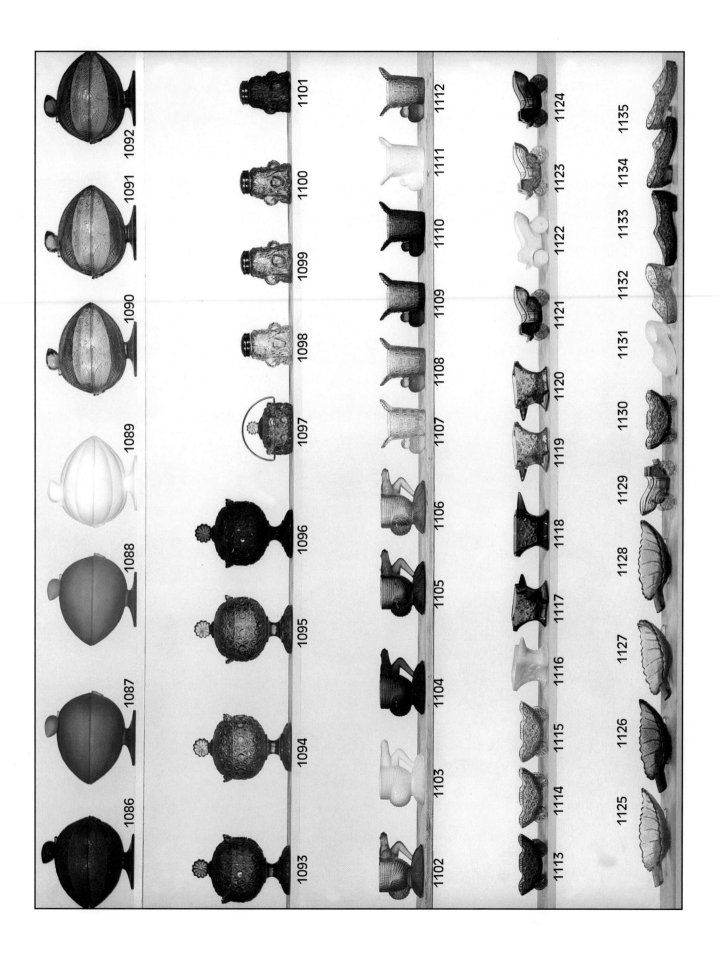

133

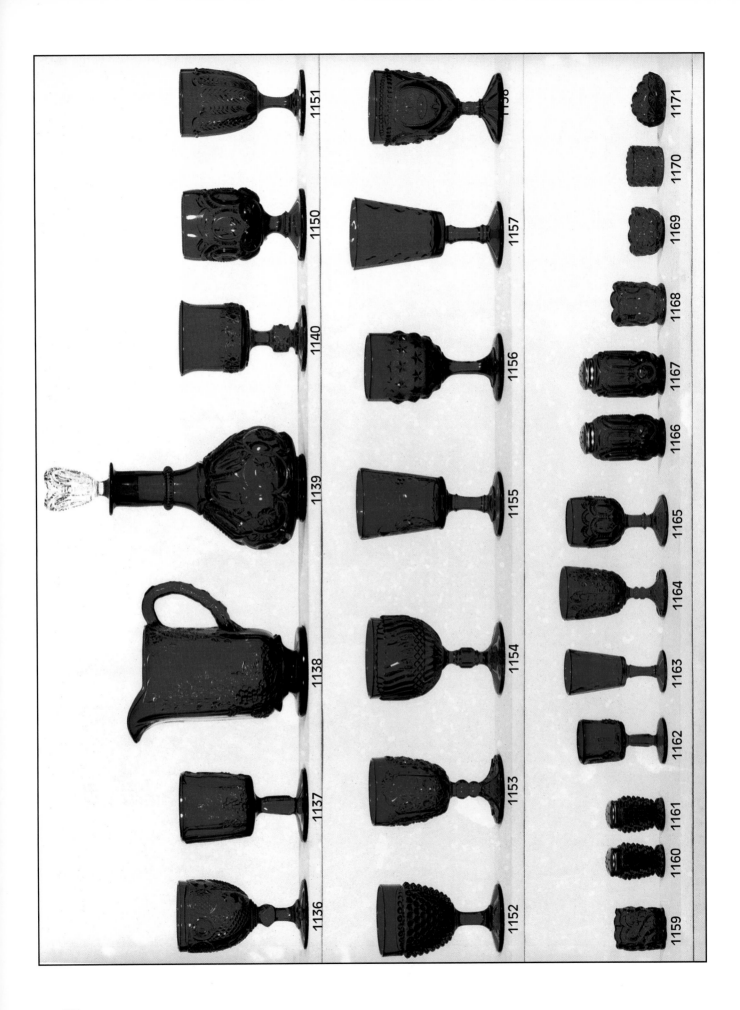

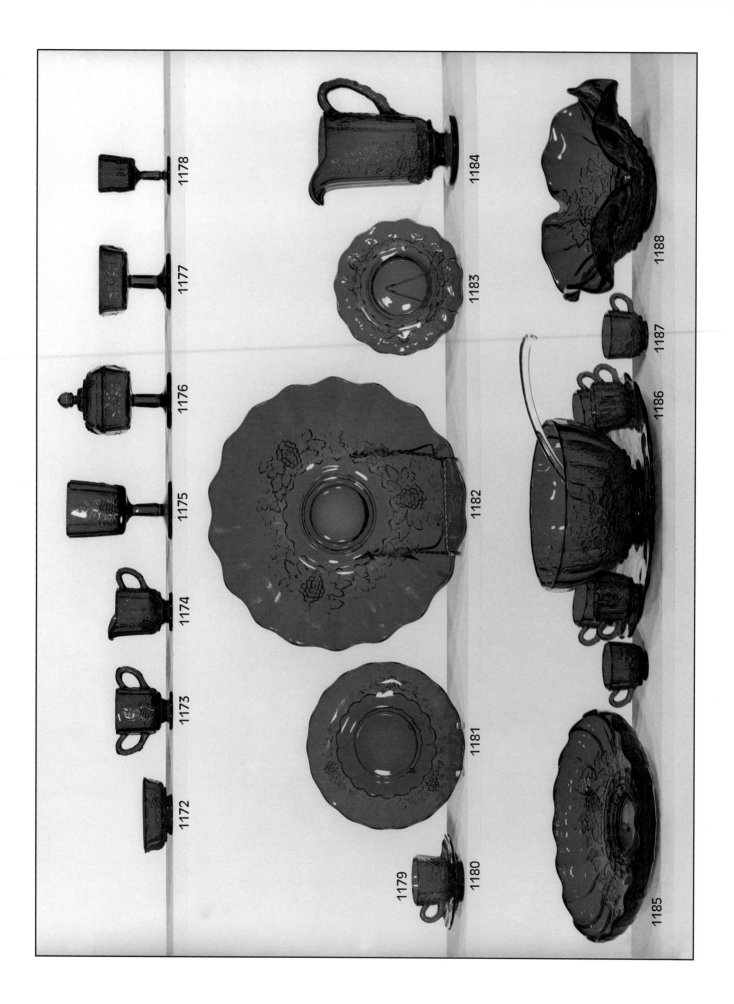

1172
1173
1174
1175
1176
1177
1178
1179
1180
1181
1182
1183
1184
1185
1186
1187
1188

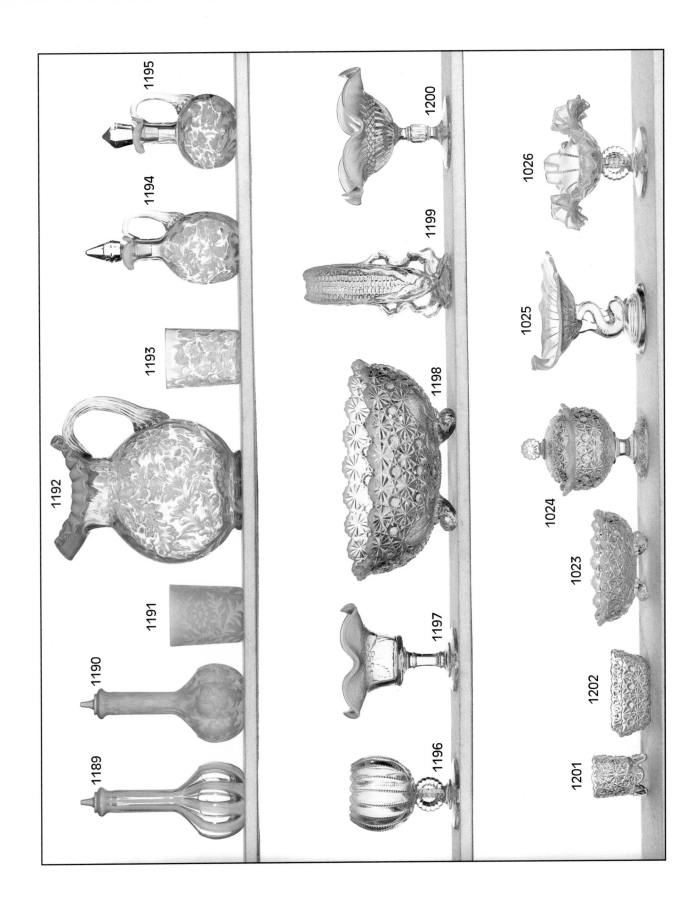

1189
1190
1191
1192
1193
1194
1195
1196
1197
1198
1199
1200
1201
1202
1023
1024
1025
1026

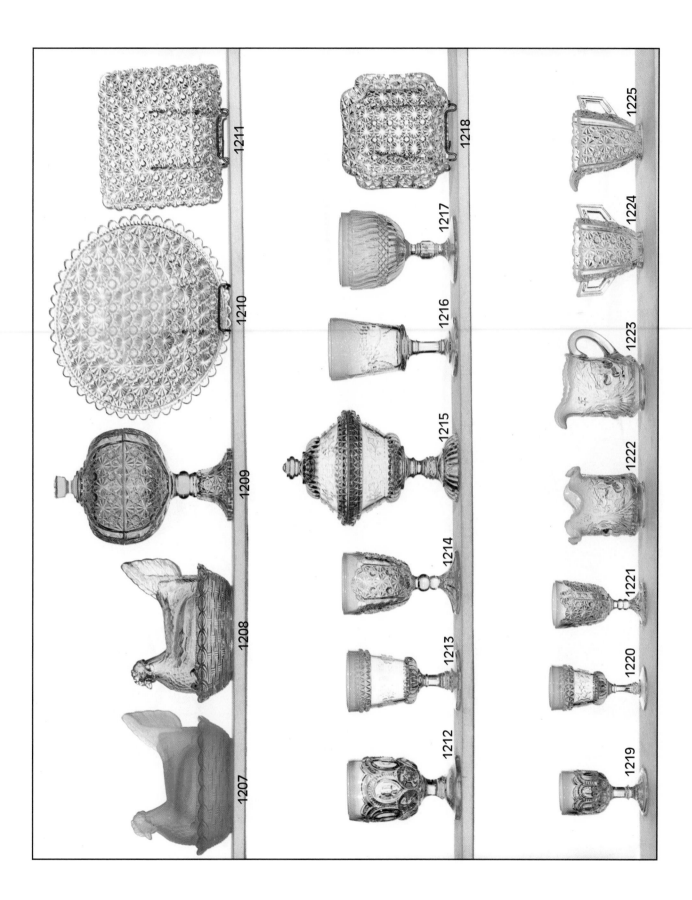

1207

1208

1209

1210

1211

1212

1213

1214

1215

1216

1217

1218

1219

1220

1221

1222

1223

1224

1225

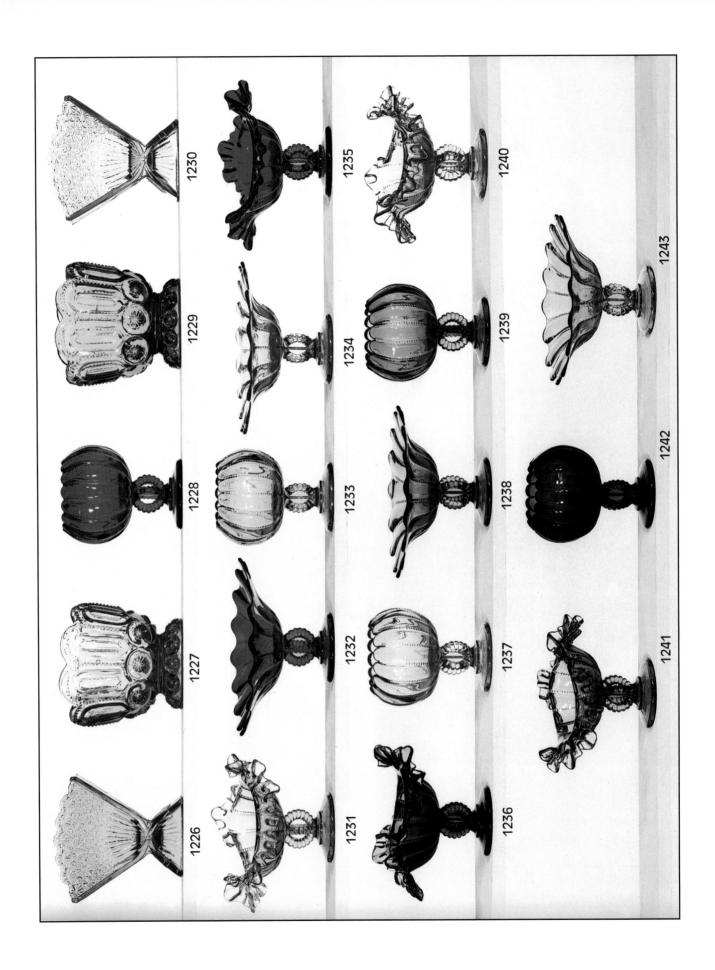

1226

1227

1228

1229

1230

1231

1232

1233

1234

1235

1236

1237

1238

1239

1240

1241

1242

1243

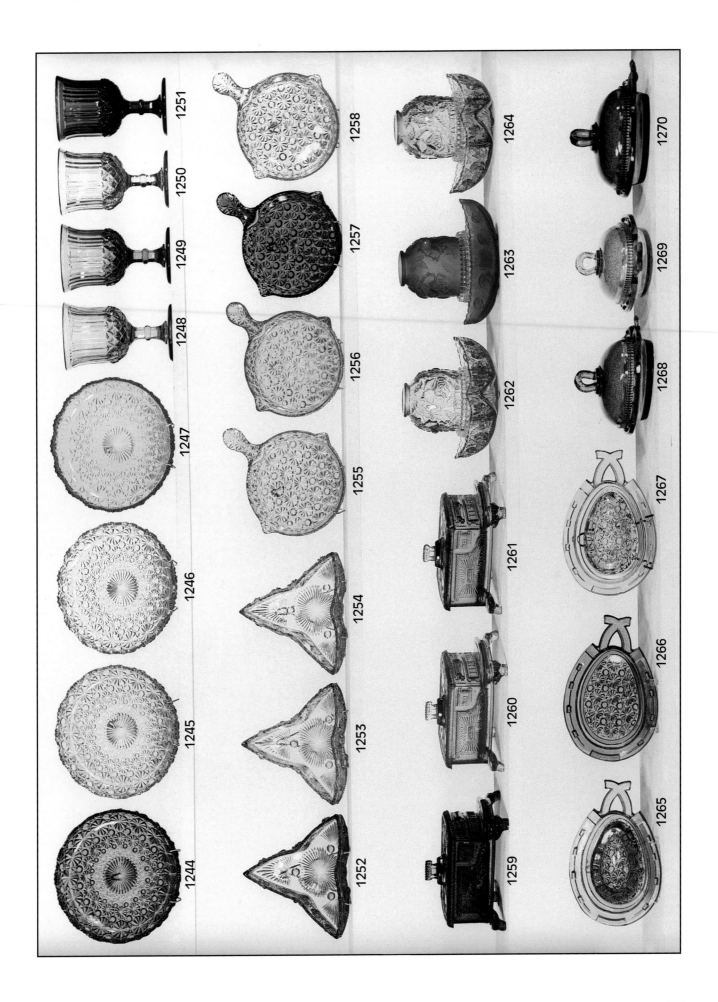

1251

1250

1249

1248

1247

1246

1245

1244

1258

1257

1256

1255

1254

1253

1252

1264

1263

1262

1261

1260

1259

1270

1269

1268

1267

1266

1265

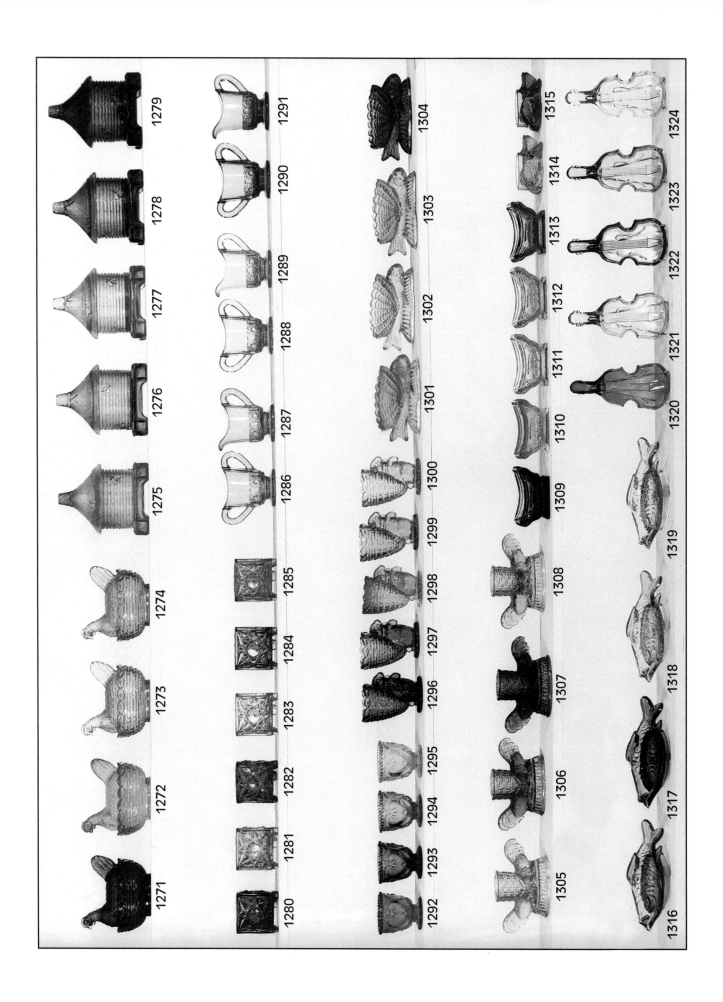

1271 1272 1273 1274 1275 1276 1277 1278 1279

1280 1281 1282 1283 1284 1285 1286 1287 1288 1289 1290 1291

1292 1293 1294 1295 1296 1297 1298 1299 1300 1301 1302 1303 1304

1305 1306 1307 1308 1309 1310 1311 1312 1313 1314 1315

1316 1317 1318 1319 1320 1321 1322 1323 1324

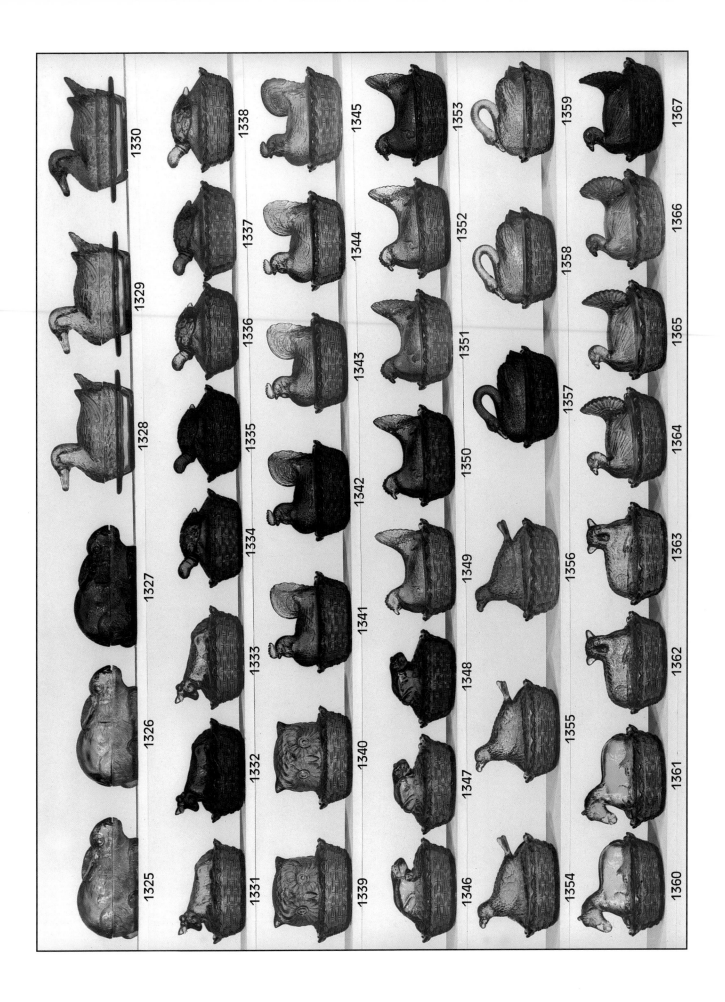

1325

1326

1327

1328

1329

1330

1331

1332

1333

1334

1335

1336

1337

1338

1339

1340

1341

1342

1343

1344

1345

1346

1347

1348

1349

1350

1351

1352

1353

1354

1355

1356

1357

1358

1359

1360

1361

1362

1363

1364

1365

1366

1367

141

1371

1374

1378

1370

1373

1377

1369

1372

1376

1368

1375

142

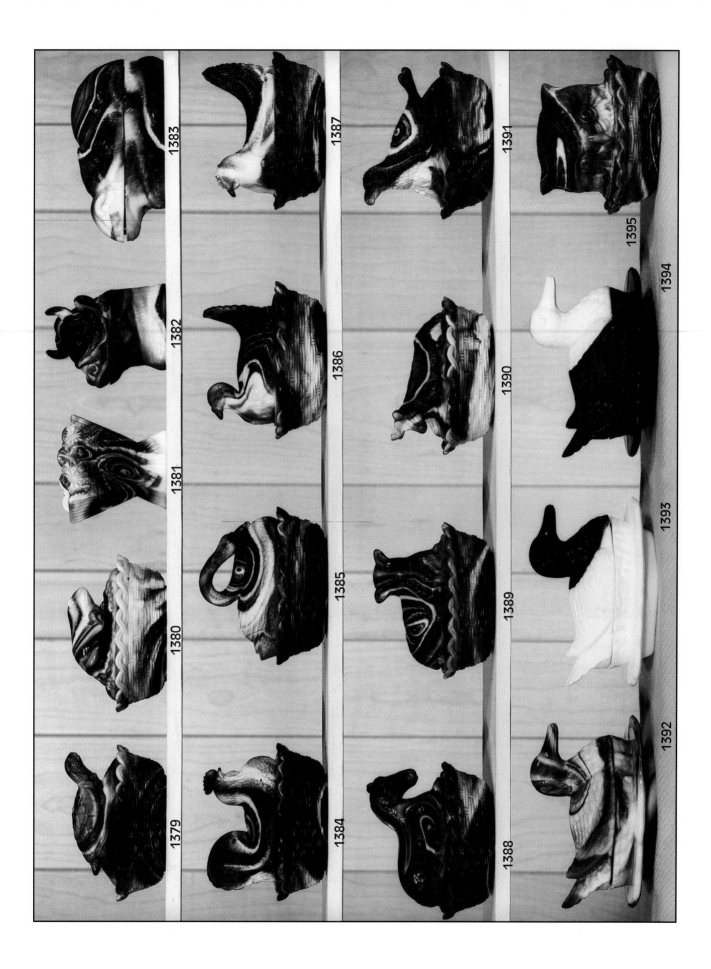

143

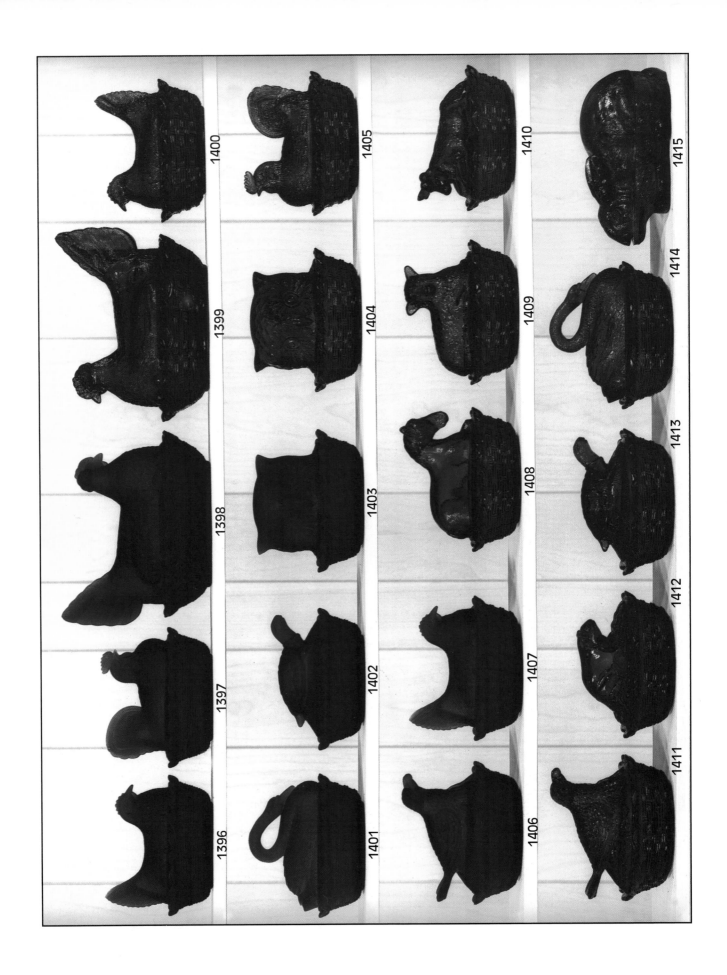

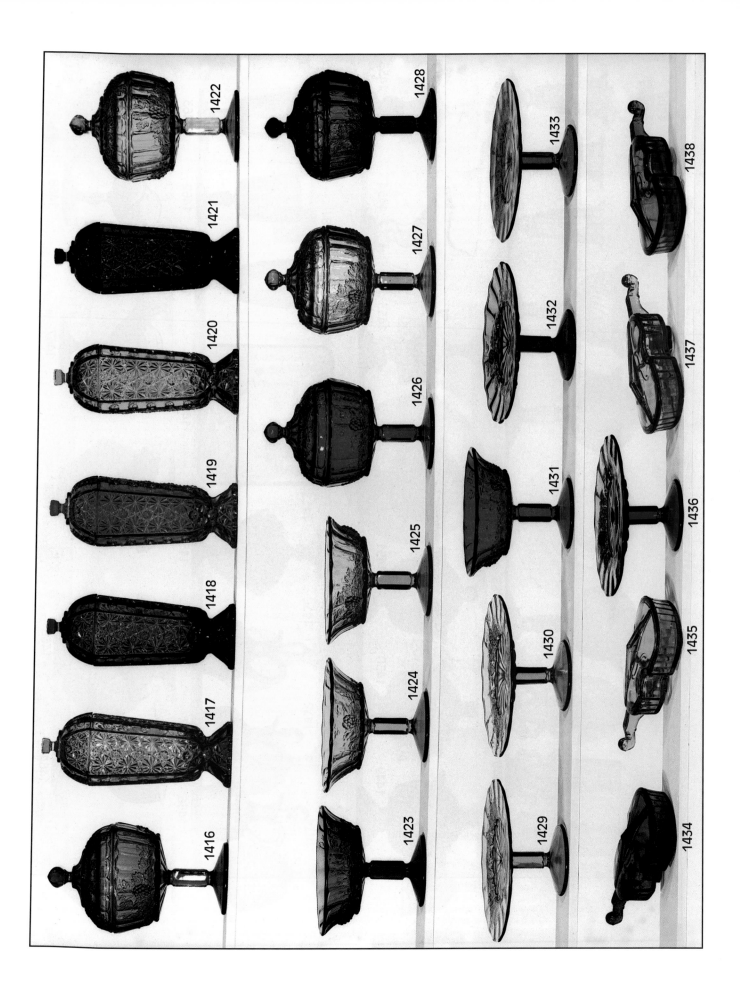

1416 1417 1418 1419 1420 1421 1422

1423 1424 1425 1426 1427 1428

1429 1430 1431 1432 1433

1434 1435 1436 1437 1438

1839

1840

1841

1842

1843

1844

1845

1846

1847

1848

1849

1850

1851

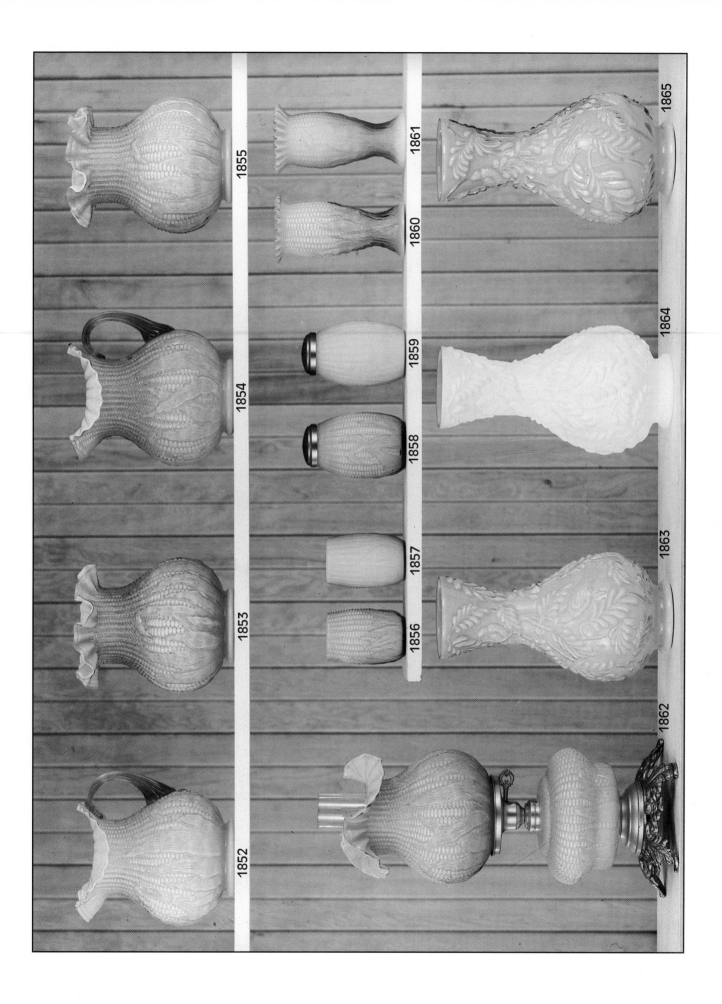

1852

1853

1854

1855

1856

1857

1858

1859

1860

1861

1862

1863

1864

1865

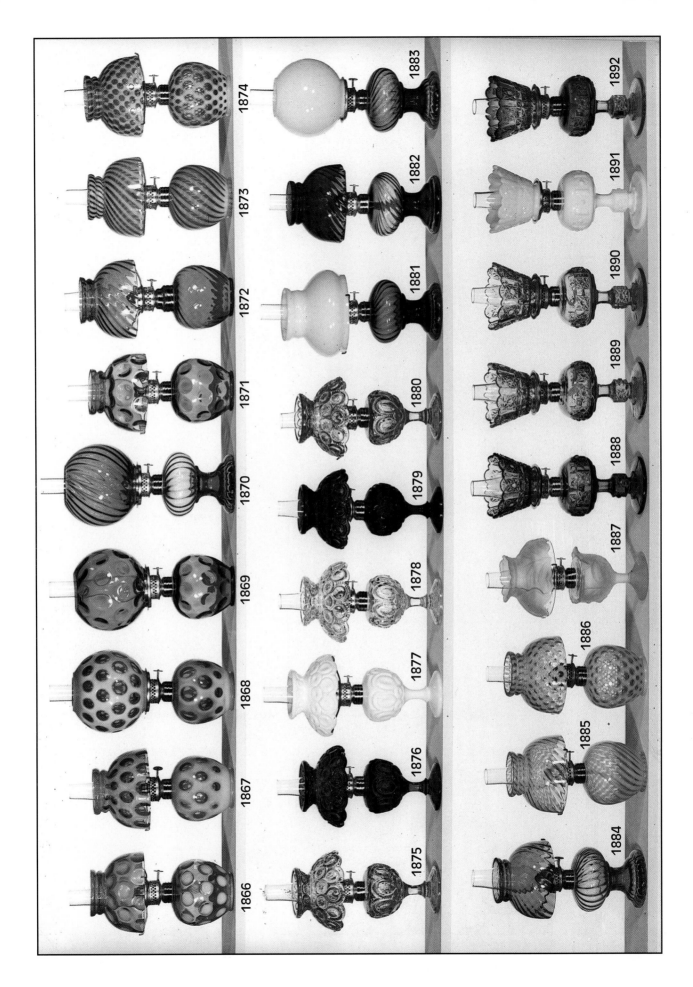

Text continued from page 77.

99-41 14" slim vase dec. Blue Holland Rose

99-42 round candy box and cover dec. Brown Apple

99-43 13" ball shape vase dec. Brown Apple

99-44 13" ball shape vase dec. Poppy

99-45 6" apothecary jar dec. Brown Apple

99-46 8" apothecary jar dec. Brown Apple

99-47 10" apothecary jar dec. Brown Apple

99-48 6" apothecary jar dec. Paisley

99-49 8" apothecary jar dec. Paisley

99-50 10" apothecary jar dec. Paisley

99-51 round candy box and cover dec. Paisley

99-52 round candy box and cover dec. Polynesian Rose

99-53 round candy box and cover dec. Mallow Rose

99-54 13" ball shape vase dec. Polynesian Rose

99-55 13" ball shape vase dec. Mallow Rose

99-56 13" ball shape vase dec. Paisley

99-57 14" slim vase dec. Mallow Rose

99-58 14" slim vase dec. Polynesian Rose

99-59 13" pear shape vase dec. Moss Rose

99-60-GRR 7" fluted vase dec. Golden Rambling Rose

99-60-SR 7" fluted vase dec. Sunset Rose

99-60-MP 7" fluted vase dec. Mountain Poppy

99-61 round candy box and cover dec. Mountain Poppy

99-62 14" slim vase dec. Mountain Poppy

99-63 13" ball shape vase dec. Mountain Poppy

99-64 round candy box and cover dec. Antique Golden Poppy

99-65 round candy box and cover dec. Pastel Poppy

99-66 14" slim vase dec. Pastel Poppy

WEDDING BOWLS

These originated about 1966-67, when an L. G. Wright price list made this announcement: "We are proud to offer to our customers, for the first time, a series of beautifully designed wedding bowls." These came in three sizes (9" 11" and 13"), but no colors were specified, although the initial announcement alluded to "delicate and beautiful hand painted floral designs."

The 1968 Wright Master Catalog showed these colors: amber overlay (also called butterscotch); blue overlay; green overlay (also called mint green); milk glass; and pink overlay. Some of these were decorated with various motifs (Bouquet, Grape, Holland Rose, Spring Flowers, Toy Rose, Yellow Rose etc.) and were available as "bride's baskets" or were mounted on metal pedestals.

101 13" wedding bowl, butterscotch

102 13" wedding bowl mint green overlay

103 13" wedding bowl blue overlay

104 13" wedding bowl milk glass

105 13" wedding bowl pink overlay

106 11" bowl crimpt top, butterscotch

107 11" crimpt bowl mint green overlay

108 11" crimpt bowl blue overlay

[109 not used]

110 9" bowl crimpt top, butterscotch

111 9" crimpt bowl mint green overlay

112 9" crimpt bowl blue overlay

113 11" crimpt bowl milk glass

114 9" crimpt bowl milk glass

115 11" crimpt bowl pink overlay

116 9" crimpt bowl pink overlay

BEADED CURTAIN

Sometimes identified only as "Beaded" in the Wright files, this small group of short-lived blown ware items was made in the late 1940s and early 1950s, although a few articles were in the line longer. Some of the moulds (creamer and lamp shade) were made at Weishar's Island Mould and Machine Co. in 1948. Some items in this pattern were sold by the John Marshall Wholesale House of Centralia, Illinois, about 1950-51.

The Beaded Curtain group (see p. 92) includes these items: cream, two-handled open sugar bowl, spooner, rose bowl, two sizes of tumblers, a tall pitcher, and a crimped-top vase as well as several lamps, including a toy lamp. Apparently, only two transparent colors were made, cranberry and dark emerald green. The opaque colors (blue, green and yellow) are vivid, and the opal-cased overlay colors (blue, green, Peach Blow, and yellow) are even more impressive, especially in the large items such as the tall pitcher.

BICENTENNIAL BELL

This item is shown as 1776-B in the 1976 Supplement.

BLUE OPALESCENT

This color was revived in the 1978 supple-

Peach Blow Beaded Curtain lamps.

ment with an offering that also employed many of the same shapes made for the Koscherak Brothers during WWII. The blue was a bit darker [note: blue opalescent Fern was also being made during this time]. The 2-1 Dahlia water pitcher and 2-2 Dahlia tumbler were made, along with many articles from the No. 7 Cherry line and some novelties such as the 77-95 Pump, the 77-96 Trough and the 77-121 Corn vase. Two especially interesting items were added in the 1981 Supplement: the 84-8 water pitcher and the 97-11 tumbler in Eye Dot and Daisy.

CABBAGE LEAF

This interesting motif was shown in black and white in a photograph taken about 1950 (see next page). These were available in amber, blue, emerald green, and crystal and each of these hues could also be ordered in "satin" finish. In 1955, a toy lamp and a 10" plate were also in the Wright line.

The covered compote was re-named after 1962 as the "70-1 Cabbage Leaf satin covered candy box," but the goblet (77-19) and wine (77-70) were the only other items which remained in the line (the wine was in John Marshall catalogs in 1980). In *Identifying Pattern Glass Reproductions*, the authors list articles (celery vase, water pitcher, etc.) allegedly made by Wright and suggest that the entire Cabbage Leaf line dates c. 1968-70; this is not correct.

Top row, left to right: covered compote, footed bowl, wine, sherbet, and goblet. Bottom row, left to right: open compote, bon bon, mint or small sherbet, and footed cake salver.

CARNIVAL GLASS

Although Si Wright wanted very much to market Carnival glass, he was not able to do so during his lifetime. However, Mrs. Wright persevered and the first Wright Carnival glass (produced by Westmoreland) debuted in the mid-1970s. A number of old Dugan moulds were used for Wright's Carnival line, including Maple Leaf, God and Home, and Stork and Rushes.

The four-piece Maple Leaf table set appeared in 1974 along with the tumbler. God and Home and Stork and Rushes appeared the next year. The latter was available in both "dark Carnival" glass and marigold carnival glass, but Maple Leaf and God and Home were produced in dark carnival only at this time. The Pony bowl and plate (made from an old Dugan mould) were available in 1976.

By 1977, the phrase dark Carnival had become "purple Carnival" in Wright's sales materials, and two new pastel Carnival hues—Ice blue Carnival and White Carnival—were also offered. Both the 2-1 Dahlia water pitcher and the 2-2 Dahlia tumbler (old Dugan moulds) were available in all three colors (note: the Dahlia moulds are now leased to the Mosser Glass Company, and green iridescent pieces have recently been marketed).

Other Carnival items in the Wright line include the following items:

4-1 Grape decanter, purple Carnival only (also crystal)
4-2 Grape wine, purple Carnival only (also crystal)
5-1 Iris water pitcher, purple Carnival only
5-2 Iris tumbler, purple Carnival only
8-1 Floral and Grape water pitcher purple Carnival only
8-2 Floral and Grape tumbler purple Carnival only
9-1 Banded Grape water pitcher purple Carnival only
9-2 Banded Grape tumbler purple Carnival only
12-1 Grape Vine Lattice water pitcher purple Carnival only
12-2 Grape Vine Lattice tumbler purple Carnival only
24-1 Sweetheart Cherry 7" round bowl purple Carnival only
70-8 7" Hen purple Carnival only
77-95 pump, purple Carnival only
77-96 trough, purple Carnival only
800-3 Rambler Rose tumbler purple Carnival only
800-4 Rambler Rose water pitcher purple Carnival only

Amethyst Carnival 1994-95

1776T

1776WP

22-59

22-58

78-2

Above: 22-50 Daisy & Button small slipper; 22-58 Daisy & Button medium slipper; 1776T God & Home tumblers; 1776 WP God & Home water pitcher; and 78-2 Stork & Rushes bowl.

Right: 820-3 Peacock bowl.

805-1 12" Grape and Fruit bowl purple Carnival only

805-3 14" Grape and Fruit plate purple Carnival only

905 Grape and Daisy tumbler purple Carnival only

920 Grape tumbler purple Carnival only (this has Cherry on the interior and Sweetheart/Jeweled Heart on the exterior)

Several noteworthy Carnival colors appeared in Wright's 1980 Supplement, including ruby Carnival, Ice Pink and Ice Green. The 70-8 7" Hen was made in both hues, but the rest of the Ice Pink was from the Thistle pattern: 64-16, 64-19, 64-22,

64-23, and 64-24. The Ice Green group was strongly reminiscent of "old" Carnival glass: 42-5 Maple leaf tumbler (also made in ruby Carnival); 42-6 Maple Leaf water pitcher (also made in ruby Carnival); 77-90 Grape and Cable 10" oval bowl (also made in Purple Carnival); 77-111 Grape and Cable oval bowl (also made in Purple Carnival); 77-125 Grape rose bowl (also made in Purple Carnival); 77-126 Grape nut bowl (also made in Purple Carnival); 1776-P God and Home water pitcher (also made in ruby Carnival); and 1776-T God and Home tumbler (also made in ruby Carnival).

There was no new Carnival in 1981, but the next year saw two limited edition water sets (1000 sets each) in Cobalt Carnival—God and Home and Maple Leaf. The 820-3 Peacock bowl and 820-2 Peacock plate are listed in amethyst Carnival for 1992-93.

The God and Home pitcher (1776WP) and tumblers (1776T) were made in amethyst Carnival glass for 1995, as were the 78-2 Stork and Rushes bowl and the small (22-59) and medium (22-58) Daisy and Button slippers.

CHOCOLATE GLASS

L. G. Wright's Chocolate glass made its debut in 1983. The glassware was made for Wright by the Westmoreland Glass Co. There were seven items in Argonaut (910, 921, 922, 923, 924, 924 and 927), plus some interesting novelty items: 70-5 Flat Iron, 70-8 7" Hen, 70-11 Stove, 70-12 large Turtle, 77-9 three-wheel cart, 77-75 Hoot Owl and 80-11 Rabbit (many of these were also issued in green at this time).

CHRISTMAS SNOWFLAKE

The opalescent motif was featured on the cover of the 1980 Supplement. The 84-6 and 97-9 tumbler were the only items made in cranberry opalescent. They were also made in cobalt blue opalescent (as 84-7 and 97-10 respectively), along with these:

85-12 milk pitcher
89-8 round barber bottle
90-14 tall cream
94-6 oval cruet
96-12 sugar shaker
96A-6 syrup pitcher
98-6 spooner
98-7 small rose bowl
98-9 large rose bowl
98-11 11" wedding bowl
98-16 small basket

CUSTARD GLASS

The 1969 Supplement pictured 32 articles in this new color, and several were also offered with handpainted decorations. Some were long-standing Wright pattern items from the Cherry line (7-3, 7-4, 7-5 and 7-8) or other articles (22-57, 22-58, 70-8, 80-7 and 80-10), but twenty pieces were new to the Wright line. These, plus pieces in

Wright's Chocolate glass, in an ad from 1983.

Decorated custard items.

Argonaut Shell, are in the 1973 Master Catalog. Except for the 77-110 S cup, they were assigned numbers from 800 to 825 and 900 to 920, as indicated below:

800-1 Cosmos crimpt bowl (800-1-12 decorated)

800-2 9" Cosmos plate (800-2-12 decorated)

800-3 7 oz. Cosmos tumbler [also 800-3-12 decorated]

805-1 12" Grape and Fruit bowl crimpt

805-2 10½" Grape and Fruit bowl round

805-3 Grape and Fruit plate

810-1 10" Holly bowl

810-2 12" Holly plate

820-1 11" Peacock bowl crimpt

820-2 12" Peacock plate

900 7 oz. Wheat tumbler

905 7 oz. Grape and Daisy tumbler (905-14 decorated)

910 5" Argonaut Shell oval bowl

911 11" Argonaut Shell bowl

912 Beaded Shell mug

913 tankard cream pitcher (913-17 dec. Moss Rose and 913-40 dec. Rose Vine)

914 tankard milk pitcher (914-17 dec. Moss Rose and 914-40 dec. Rose Vine)

920 6 oz. Grape tumbler (920-15 decorated)

Note : A few pieces of "satin custard ware" decorated with Moss Rose are shown in the 1975 Supplement. These were made from the same shape moulds used for cranberry glass 73-1 (sugar shaker), 73-2 (tumbler), 73-3 water pitcher, 73-4 milk pitcher, 73-5 tall cream and 930-CMR 21" lamp. These same moulds (plus the interesting 73-6 large basket with looped handle) were used for custard again in 1981; this time the decorations were Gold Floral and Strawberry.

FERN PATTERN

Generally called Daisy and Fern by collectors, this motif in blown ware is created by a spot mould. Several vaseline opalescent and vaseline satin opalescent items appear in the 1976 Supplement.

100-1 water pitcher

100-2 tumbler

100-3 ice tea

100-4 21" lamp

100-5 17" lamp

The group was expanded dramatically in the 1979 Supplement with two full pages devoted to Blue Fern and Vaseline Fern. The numbers for

the pitcher and tumblers were changed (matching the sequence used for cranberry glass), and these items were shown:

77-124 oil lamp (burner on syrup pitcher)

84-2 water pitcher

85-2 milk pitcher

88-2 fluted barber bottle

89-2 round barber bottle

90-2 tall creamer

94-2 oval cruet

95-2 round cruet

96-2 sugar shaker

96A-2 syrup pitcher

97-2 tumbler

98-2 pickle jar w/cover

98-2-103 pickle jar plain frame

98-6 small rose bowl

98-7 large rose bowl

98-8 11" wedding bowl

98-8 biscuit jar w/silver handle and cover

100-3 ice tea

725 hurricane lamp

Three more items were added in 1981:

98-10 candy box and cover

98-14 large basket with looped handle

98-16 small basket

FLAME LAMP

A small fairy light is the only article here. Several more moulds were ordered from Botson in October-November, 1962, but they were later cancelled.

FINGER BOWLS

Discontinued in the late 1950s or early 1960s, these articles were first made for Wright by Fenton in the 1930s in cranberry (thumbprint etc.) and cranberry opalescent (eye dot etc.).

GOD AND HOME

There are just two items, the water pitcher (1776-WP) and tumbler (1776-T), but they are spectacular pieces These were made from old Dugan moulds, and they were shown in the 1975 Wright Catalog Supplement in Carnival glass. A limited edition (1000 sets) of the Cobalt Carnival water set was made in 1982, and Blue Slag water sets were first marketed in 1984.

LION

In addition to the 77-28 goblet and the 77-49 bread plate (sometimes called Lion and Cable by collectors), Wright also made the Lion egg cup. All of these first appeared in the late 1930s, and the goblet and bread plate remained in the Wright line throughout the company's history.

MARY GREGORY DECORATION

These well-executed white figures on cobalt glass are first shown in the 1981 Supplement. There were five items, and each could be had with either the boy or the girl. The syrup jug was added in 1982, and all six articles were also available with a white floral motif in 1983.

    71-1 water pitcher
    71-2 tumbler
    71-3 oval cruet
    71-4 round barber bottle
    71-5 large basket with looped handle
    75-1 syrup jug (in 1982 Master Catalog)

MILK GLASS

Perhaps because of the well-established milk glass lines marketed by Fenton, Imperial and Westmoreland, L. G. Wright did little with pressed milk glass, preferring instead to make a long line of blown milk glass vases or lamps, most of which were decorated. Nonetheless, one early photo (see p. 170) depicts some pressed milk glass items.

OVERLAY GLASS

First mentioned in the 1977 Supplement, following the debut of Wildrose Satin by about a year. More shapes were added in the 1978 Supplement. These shapes were available in overlay glass (amber, amethyst, light blue and dark blue):

    1-1 barber bottle (oval shape)
    1-2 cruet (oval shape)
    1-3 fairy light
    1-4 candy box
    1-5 large rose bowl
    1-6 small rose bowl

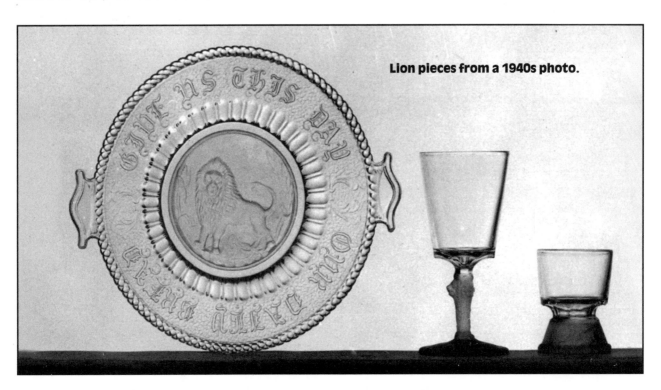

Lion pieces from a 1940s photo.

1981 Supplement
To Master Catalog

The L. G. Wright Glass Co.   New Martinsville, West Virginia 26155

Top row, left to right: Strawberry and Currant goblet and compote, vine salt and pepper shakers, Daisy and Button spooner or vase, and S cruet.
Middle row, left to right: possibly Foxglove vases , Cherry sugar and cream, Daisy and Cube compote and goblet.
Bottom row, left to right: Cherry comport, Flat Iron covered candy box, Kitten slipper, medium slipper, small slipper, Swan salt dip and Dolphin compote.

1-7 vine cruet
1-8 vine salt and pepper shakers
1-9 sugar shaker
1-10 milk pitcher
1-11 tall cream
1-12 pickle jar w/cover
1-14 spooner (pickle caster insert)
1-15 fluted cruet
1-16 round cruet
1-17 fluted barber bottle

PONY

These Carnival glass (both amethyst and marigold) pieces (23-1 crimped bowl and 23-2 9" plate), which appeared in the 1976 Supplement, were made from the old Dugan mould, part of the group purchased in Indiana, Pa., in 1939.

SLAG GLASS AND SPATTER GLASS

These two treatments were new to the L. G. Wright line in 1986-87, and both were made by the Gibson Glass Co. This slag is made by gathering two colors (milk glass plus another) together on a blowpipe before the glass is shaped. The effect is described by some a that of a "marble cake" as the colors mix but do not mingle. The 1987 Wright Price List described the slag glass as "red, blue, green [or] amethyst." In addition to the items listed below, two slag paperweights (large and small), were also made as well as a small slag bird.

Spatter glass is made by rolling the gather of glass in color "frit" (fine chips) before the piece takes its final shape. The frit flattens and expands when the article is blown, and the effect resembles the droplets of a liquid "spatter." The 1987 Wright Price List described the spatter glass as "amethyst, light blue, dark blue [or] red."

Nine Wright items were made in various slag or spatter effects. The colors will vary considerably from item to item, and they may also display an iridescent look:

1-7 vine cruet
1-15 fluted cruet
77-130 tee pee cruet
90-2 tall cream
91-1 short cream and sugar
96-2 sugar shaker
94-6 oval cruet
98-6 small rose bowl
98-16 small basket

SWEETHEART

Once thought to be a Northwood pattern and called Jeweled Heart by collectors, this motif has now been positively linked to the Dugan Glass Co., c. 1905, where it was originally called Victor.

Wright acquired quite a few original moulds in 1939, and the cream and sugar mould were used for colored glass throughout the 1960s. In the 1978 Supplement, the 24-1 Sweetheart Cherry 7" round bowl is shown in purple Carnival (this has Cherry on the interior and Sweetheart on the exterior). This bowl is shown in Cobalt Carnival in the 1996 Wright catalog as are these items in crystal (some with gold decoration) and/or lustred Ice Crystal:

24-1 bowl
77-11 cream and sugar
77-64 toothpick
77-115 fairy lamp (crystal decorated only)
240 lamp (crystal decorated only)

Sweetheart pieces from the 1994 Wright catalog.

THOUSAND EYE

Both the goblet (later numbered 77-43) and the square plate in this pattern were introduced early in 1941. They were first made in crystal along with blue, amber and apple green, but vaseline (also called yellow or canary) was soon added. Both goblets and plates in these colors were still in the line about 1950, and they appear in the Supplement to the John Marshall Wholesale House's 1949-50 catalog.

WILDROSE

There are these items: 70-16 tall covered compote, 77-41 goblet, 77-69, wine [Botson mould 7/30/62], 77-73 ice tea 77-78 8" three-toed nappy, 77-86 7" ash tray, 77-87 6" ash tray, 77-88 4" ash tray, 77-89 three-piece ash tray set, and 77-97 large goblet.

WRIGHT PLATE

Just a few days after Si Wright's death in 1969, Albert Botson completed work on the mould for this oval plate, which is called the L. G. Wright Emblem plate. This article is shown in the photo above, along with the old building on the Wright family farm (inset). It seems fitting to end this book with such a picture.

COLOR PAGE CAPTIONS

page 81
This cranberry opalescent motif was simply called "fern" by Wright, but collectors today refer to it as "Daisy and Fern." **1.** Water pitcher, c. 1940s. **2.** Water pitcher, c. 1940s. **3.** 84-2 water pitcher (satin-finished). **4.** 84-2 water pitcher. **5.** 85-2 milk pitcher (satin-finished). **6.** 85-2 milk pitcher. **7.** 98-2 pickle caster (w/feet). **8.** 96A-2 syrup jug fitted with lamp burner. **9.** 96A-2 syrup pitcher. **10.** 88-2 barber bottle. **11.** 88-2 barber bottle (satin-finished). **12.** Large hat (not in line). **13.** 90-2 tall cream. **14.** Finger bowl, c. 1950s-early 1960s. **15.** Rose bowl. **16.** 94-2 oval cruet. **17.** 95-2 round cruet.

page 82
These are Wright's cranberry "swirl" motif unless otherwise indicated. **18.** Ice tea (satin-finished). **19.** Ice tea. **20.** 97-4 tumbler. **21.** 84-4 water pitcher. **22.** 96-4 sugar shaker. **23.** Vase, c. 1950s. **24.** 98-4 pickle jar. **25.** 10-4 toy lamp with half shade. **26.** 90-4 tall cream. **27.** 11-4 toy lamp with ball shade. **28.** 96A-4 syrup pitcher (satin-finished). **29.** Finger bowl, c. 1950s-early 1960s. **30.** 88-4 barber bottle. **31.** 88-4 barber bottle. **32.** 85-4 milk pitcher (swirls are wider than usual). **33.** 85-9 milk pitcher w/rib (heavy opalescent effect; not in the line this way. **34.** 84-4 milk pitcher (satin-finished). **35.** 88-6 barber bottle w/eye dot. **36.** 88-6 barber bottle w/eye dot. **37.** Finger bowl w/eye dot. **38.** 97-6 tumbler w/eye dot. **39.** Sample milk pitcher (dot and mitre; not in line). **40.** Crimped finger bowl w/eye dot. **41.** 92-6 fluted cruet w/eye dot. **42.** 90-6 tall cream w/eye dot (satin-finished).

page 83
These cranberry items are Wright's "dot" motif (top two rows), stars and stripes motif (third row) and others as indicated. **43.** 98-3 pickle jar. **44.** 85-3 milk pitcher. **45.** 84-3 water pitcher. **46.** 97-3 tumbler. **47.** Water pitcher, c. 1950s. **48.** Crimped finger bowl. **49.** 10-6 toy lamp w/half shade. **50.** Finger bowl. **51.** 90-3 tall cream. **52.** 95-3 round cruet. **53.** Finger bowl, stars and stripes motif. **54.** 96A-8 syrup pitcher, stars and stripes motif. **55.** 94-8 oval cruet, stars and stripes motif. **56-57-58.** 97-8 tumblers, stars and stripes motif. **59.** 97-5 tumbler w/honeycomb. **60.** Finger bowl w/honeycomb. **61.** Milk pitcher w/drapery. **62.** Barber bottle w/drapery.

page 84
63. Water pitcher, swirl. **64.** Vase, rib. **65.** 84-7 water pitcher, quilted. **66.** Water pitcher, quilted, square mouth. **67.** 84-11 water pitcher, swirl. **68.** 85- 11 milk pitcher, swirl. **69.** 90-7 tall cream, quilted. **70.** 85-7 milk pitcher quilted. **71.** Vase w/swirl. **72.** 90-11 all cream w/swirl. **73.** 95-11 round cruet w/swirl. **74.** 95-11 round cruet w/swirl (satin-finished). **75-76.** 91-7 short sugar and cream, quilted. **77-78-79.** Samples of 85-9 milk pitcher w/rib.

page 85
All of these cranberry glass items are Wright's thumbprint motif. **80.** 75-5 vase, crimpt top. **81.** 99-5 ball shape vase. **82.** 84-1 water pitcher (note plain handle). **83.** 84-1 water pitcher. **84.** Water pitcher. **85.** 11-1 toy lamp, ball shade (satin-finished). **86.** 10-3 toy lamp, half shade. **87.** 87-1 large oval apothecary jar. **88.** 86-1 medium oval apothecary jar. **89.** 6" apothecary jar. **90.** Ice tea. **91.** Vase. **92.** Syrup pitcher. **93.** 85-1 milk pitcher. **94.** vase. **95.** finger bowl. **96.** 96-1 sugar shaker. **97.** 89-1 barber bottle, fluted. **98.** barber bottle, round. **99-100.** 91-1 short sugar and short cream. **101.** 94-1 oval cruet. **102.** 95-1 round cruet. **103.** 93-1 fluted vine cruet. **104.** 92-1 fluted cruet.

page 86
Fern motif. **105.** vase. **106.** vase. **107.** vase. **108.** vase. **109.** 87-2 large oval apothecary jar. **110.** 6" apothecary jar. **111.** 10" apothecary jar. **112.** 8" apothecary jar. **113.** 86-2 medium oval apothecary jar

(satin-finished). **114.** 86-2 medium oval apothecary jar. **115.** 8" apothecary jar (satin-finished). **116.** sample vase. **117.** 96-2 sugar shaker. **118.** 97-2 tumbler. **119.** 97-2 tumbler. **120.** 97-2 tumbler. **121.** 97-2 tumbler (satin-finished).

page 87

This motif was called "honeycomb" by Wright. **122.** Vase. **123.** 97-5 tumbler. **124.** 84-5 water pitcher. **125.** 97-5 tumbler. **126.** 84-5 water pitcher (note darker color). **127.** 94-5 cruet. **128.** 11-5 toy lamp. ball shade. **129.** 90-5 tall cream. **130.** 10-5 toy lamp. half shade. **131.** 85-5 milk pitcher. **132.** Bowl. **133.** 96A-5 syrup pitcher. **134.** 96A-5 syrup pitcher. **135.** Finger bowl. This motif was called "rib" by Wright. **136.** 94-10 oval cruet. **137.** 88-10 barber bottle. **138.** 85-10 milk pitcher. **139.** Rose bowl.

page 88

140. Cranberry epergne with swirl. **141.** Cranberry lamp with rib and Snow Crest edge. **142.** Cranberry epergne. **143.** Cranberry epergne with Snow Crest edge. **144.** Cranberry epergne with honeycomb (satin finish). **145.** Cranberry lamp with honeycomb (satin finish). **146.** Cranberry vase with thumbprint and Snow Crest edge. **147.** Cranberry Maize 40-2 rose bowl (satin finish). **148.** Cranberry Maize 40-2 rose bowl.

page 89

149. Cranberry epergne with fern. **150.** Cranberry barber bottle with stars and stripes. **151.** Cranberry small epergne. **152.** Cranberry Beaded Curtain pitcher. **153.** 24-1 Sweetheart purple Carnival glass bowl (Cherries interior). **154.** Ruby Sweetheart oval bowl. **155.** 240 Sweetheart lamp. **156.** Amber Sweetheart plate (Cherries interior). **157.** Amber 77-115A Sweetheart fairy lamp. **158.** Decorated 77-11 Sweetheart crystal sugar with cover. **159.** Ruby 77-11 Sweetheart cream. **160-161.** Amber 77-107 Mirror and Rose salt and pepper shakers. **162.** Green 77-115G Sweetheart fairy lamp. **163.** Ruby 77-82 Sweetheart wine. **164.** Amber Sweetheart sauce. **165.** Blue Sweetheart tumbler. **166.** Ruby 77-64 Sweetheart toothpick. **167.** Amber 77-37 Sweetheart goblet.

page 90

168. Cranberry three-part lamp, swirl motif. **169.** Cranberry lamp (swirl motif) with milk glass base. **170.** Cranberry lamp (honeycomb motif) with milk glass base. **171.** Large Cranberry (eye dot motif) lamp. **172.** Probably not an L. G. Wright lamp.

page 91

173. Cranberry three-part lamp, honeycomb motif (satin finish). **174.** Cranberry lamp, fern motif. **175.** Cranberry lamp, fern motif. **176.** Cranberry lamp, dot motif (satin finish). **177.** Christmas Snowflake cranberry lamp.

page 92

Wright's Beaded Curtain was made in the 1940s and 1950s, although various lamps (especially cranberry) remained in the line for many years. **178.** green cream (satin-finished). **179.** yellow overlay pitcher. **180.** green overlay lamp. **181.** blue overlay vase. **182.** green overlay vase. **183.** Peach Blow pickle jar insert. **184.** Peach Blow tumbler. **185.** Peach Blow sugar. **186.** Peach Blow cream. **187.** Peach Blow spooner. **188.** Peach Blow rose bowl. **189.** green overlay pitcher. **190.** Peach Blow pitcher. **191.** yellow overlay pitcher.

page 93

Wright's epergnes were very popular in the 1940s and 1950s. These were made by Fenton, of course, and each epergne has a large central straight cone and three smaller curved cones. **192.** Milk glass with blue crest (Fenton called this Aqua Crest). **193.** Blue opalescent with crystal crest. **194.** Milk glass with pink crest (Fenton called this Rose Crest). **195.** Milk glass with amber crest (Fenton called this Gold Crest) **196.** Vaseline opalescent with crystal crest. **197.** Milk glass with amethyst crest.

page 94

198. Peach Blow vase. **199.** green overlay vase. **200.** Peach Blow picture vase. **201.** Peach Blow round cruet, decorated Moss Rose. **202.** Peach Blow epergne (note snow crest). **203.** Peach Blow pickle jar, decorated Moss Rose. **204.** opal epergne with peach crest. **205.** Peach Blow vase, decorated Moss Rose. **206.** Peach Blow barber bottle. **207.** Peach Blow vase (made from barber bottle). **208.** Peach Blow pitcher. **209.** Peach Blow decorated Cherry vase. **210.** Peach Blow Cherry vase. **211.** Peach Blow finger bowl with crimped edge. **212.** Peach Blow decorated tumbler. **213.** Peach Blow decorated tumbler. **214.** Peach Blow small rose bowl (satin finished). **215.** Peach Blow large rose bowl. **216.** Peach Blow small rose bowl.

page 95

Wright's decorated Moss Rose items were popular for many years, especially on Peach Blow glass. **217, 219** and **220.** Peach Blow vase, tumbler and pitcher. **218.** Milk glass lattice open edge plate. **221-222.** Peach blow picture vases (note reverse side). **223.** Peach Blow cream. **224.** Peach Blow vase. **225.** Milk glass syrup jug. **226.** Peach Blow fairy lamp. **227.** Peach Blow rose bowl. **228.** Peach Blow large rose bowl. **229.** Peach Blow rose bowl. **230.** Peach Blow pickle caster. **231.** Peach Blow cruet.

page 96

Wright lamps with decorated Moss Rose. **232.** Peach Blow lamp. **233.** Peach Blow three-part lamp. **234.** Milk glass lamp with ball shade. **235.** Milk glass lamp with half shade. **236.** Peach Blow toy lamp.

page 97

Some of these early (c. late 1940s-early 1950s) decorated items could be the work of the Zarilla Art Glass Company, which decorated glass for L. G. Wright. **237.** milk glass lattice open edge plate with blackberry decoration. **238.** milk glass lattice open edge plate with grape decoration. **239.** milk glass lattice open edge plate with cattails decoration. **240.** milk glass lattice closed edge plate. **241.** purple slag lattice closed edge plate. **242.** crystal lattice closed edge plate. **243.** milk glass swirl plate with floral decoration. **244.** milk glass swirl plate with floral decoration. **245.** milk glass lattice open edge plate, made into shallow bowl.

page 98

246. custard Fisherman mug. **247.** milk glass 77-60 Frog toothpick. **248.** milk glass Ivy in Snow celery vase (bought from the Phoenix Glass Co. and first sold by Wright in the 1930s). **249.** milk glass S cruet (later 77-12). **250.** milk glass S toothpick (later 77-63). **251.** crystal Hobnail sugar shaker. **252.** milk glass Hobnail sugar shaker. **253.** ruby Moon and Star syrup pitcher. **254.** blue Daisy and Button wall planter. **255.** ruby Hobnail sugar shaker. **256.** amber Hobnail sugar shaker. **257.** dark blue 70-15 Embossed Rose four-toed candy box and cover. **258.** dark 77-78 Embossed Rose three-toed 9" nappy. **259.** amber overlay Moon and Star whimsey vase (not in line; made from syrup pitcher).

page 99

Many of these blue opalescent Wright Panel Grape items were sold to the Kosherak Bros. New York City firm in the early 1950s. **260.** punch bowl with ladle. **261.** underplate for punch bowl. **262.** punch cup **263.** lily bowl. **264.** crimpt bowl. **265.** epergne set (2 pcs.). **266.** goblet. **267.** pitcher. **268.** bowl. **269.** sherbet. **270.** wine. **271.** goblet. **272.** basket. **273.** crystal goblet with "Natural Color Decoration."

page 100

Blue opalescent items. **274.** 84-2 pitcher, fern c. 1979 (note crimped rim and color). **275.** 84-2 pitcher, fern. **276.** 98-2 pickle jar, fern. **277.** sample pitcher, fern (square mouth). 278. 89-2 barber bottle, fern. **279.** 95-2 round cruet, fern. **280.** 85-2 milk pitcher, fern. **281.** 96-2 sugar shaker, fern. **282.** 98-16 small basket, fern c. 1981. **283.** 97-2 tumbler, fern. **284.** 97-2 tumbler, fern. **285.** 90-2 tall cream, fern. **286.**

90-2 tall cream, fern c. 1979. **287.** finger bowl, fern. **288.** 88-6 barber bottle, eye dot (satin finish). **289.** 92-6 fluted cruet, eye dot. **290.** finger bowl, eye dot. **291.** 88-6 barber bottle, eye dot.

page 101

Blue opalescent items. **292.** 97-11 tumbler, Eye Dot and Daisy c. 1981. **293.** 84-8 pitcher, Eye Dot and Daisy c. 1981. **294.** tumbler. **295.** pitcher. **296.** tumbler. **297.** pitcher. **298.** toy lamp. **299.** tall cream, quilted. **300.** vase. **301.** finger bowl, Swirl. **302.** tall cream, Swirl. **303.** milk pitcher, Rib. **304.** finger bowl, Honeycomb (satin finish). **305.** oval cruet, honeycomb. **306.** fluted barber bottle, swirl. **307.** blue Hobnail barber bottle (not opalescent). **308.** 97-8 tumbler, stars and stripes. **309.** 97-3 tumbler, dot. **310.** 96-10 sugar shaker, rib. **311.** finger bowl, dot.

page 102

Blue opalescent items. **312.** whimsey made from 3-5 Beaded large ivy bowl. **313.** 3-3 Beaded large footed compote, flared. **314.** 70/72- Dolphin open compote. **315.** blue epergne (large central straight cone and three smaller curved cones) with milk glass crest. **316.** early Cherry deep bowl. **317-318.** Corn vases (note different colors and opalescent effects). **319.** Pump. **320.** Trough. **321.** early Cherry deep bowl. **322.** early Cherry round bowl. **323.** early Cherry bowl **324.** early Cherry crimped bowl.

page 103

Blue opalescent items, Cherry c. 1978 and Argonaut c. 1970. **325.** 7-12 Cherry goblet. **326.** 7-15 Cherry ice tea. **327.** 7-9 Cherry tumbler. **328.** 7-10/14 Cherry water pitcher. **329.** 7-5 Cherry sugar. **330-331.** 7-4 Cherry creams (note differences in color and opalescence). **332.** 7-8 Cherry toothpick. **333.** 7-4 Cherry sugar (note unusual crimp). **334.** 7-17 Cherry 5" oval bowl. **335.** 7-2 Cherry butter and cover. **336.** 2-2 Dahlia tumbler. **337.** 923 Argonaut sugar (base). **338.** 910 Argonaut 5" Shell bowl. **339.** 921 Argonaut butter and cover. **340.** 924 Argonaut stemmed jelly. **341.** 922 Argonaut cream. **342.** 926 Argonaut tumbler. **343.** 925 Argonaut toothpick. **344-345.** 927 Argonaut salt and pepper shakers. **346.** 33-7 Hobnail finger bowl, crimpt. **347.** Hobnail shallow bowl with crimped edge. **348.** 33-9 Hobnail rose bowl, crimpt.

page 104

Blue and blue opalescent items. **349.** Moon and Star 8" covered compote. **350.** Moon and Star 10" open compote. **351.** Moon and Star whimsey vase (not in line). **352.** Moon and Star bowl. **353.** Moon and Star low covered compote. **354.** Moon and Star goblet with crimped edge. **355.** Moon and Star toy lamp. **356.** crystal epergne (large central straight cone and three smaller curved cones) with blue crest. **357.** 60-9 Tree of Life footed crimpt compote. **358.** 60-3 Tree of Life finger bowl. **359.** Shell and Tassel covered compote. **360.** Cabbage Leaf covered compote (satin finish). **361.** 77-7 Chick covered basket. **362.** 5-2 Beaded Grape oil bottle or cruet. **363.** Daisy and Cube toy lamp. **364.** Grape punch cup (not in line). **365.** 925 Argonaut toothpick (satin finish). **366.** 37-4 Magnet and Grape sherbet.

page 105

The "Mary Gregory" decoration (boy or girl) was introduced in the 1981 Supplement. **367.** 556 lamp. **368.** 71-2 tumbler. **369.** 71-5 large basket with looped handle. **370.** 71-6 ice tea. **371.** 71-1 water pitcher. **372-373.** 71-2 tumbler and 71-1 water pitcher with White Floral decoration c. 1983. **374.** 77-129 Chick Basket toothpick holder. **375.** Daisy and Button Fan vase. **376-377.** 71-6 ice tea and 71-6 water pitcher with White Floral decoration c. 1983. Cobalt Christmas Snowflake, introduced in the 1980 Supplement, was inspired by a c. 1899 Northwood motif: **378.** 96-9 large rose bowl. **379.** 98-11 11" Wedding bowl. **380.** 85-12 milk pitcher. **381.** 98-16 basket. **382.** 96-12 sugar shaker. **383.** 90-14 tall cream. **384.** 97-10 tumbler. **385.** 96A-6 syrup pitcher.

page 106

Vaseline opalescent was in the Wright line during the mid-1960s. **386.** 98-2 pickle jar, fern. **387.** syrup jug fitted with lamp burner. **388.** 85-2 milk pitcher, fern. **389.** 44-18 Moon and Star decanter c.

1976. **390.** 84-3 pitcher, Dot. **391.** 84-2 pitcher, fern. **392.** 88-2 fluted barber bottle, fern. **393.** 84-2 pitcher, fern. **394.** 89-2 round barber bottle, fern. **395.** 84-2 or 100-1 pitcher, fern (100-1 was made c. 1976). **396.** 96A-2 syrup pitcher, fern. **397.** 98-7 large rose bowl, fern c. 1979. **398.** 98-8 Wedding bowl, fern c. 1979. **399.** 98-9 Biscuit Jar, fern c. 1980. **400.** 88-10 fluted barber bottle, Rib. **401.** 100-3 ice tea, fern c. 1976. **402.** 90-2 tall cream, fern. **403.** 97-2 or 100-2 tumbler, fern (100-2 was made c. 1976). **404.** 96-2 sugar shaker, fern. **405.** 95-2 round cruet, fern (satin finish). **406.** 95-2 round cruet, fern.

page 107
Vaseline and vaseline opalescent. **407.** 22-19 Daisy and Button large square covered compote. **408.** 3-5 Beaded large footed ivy bowl. **409.** 3-3 Beaded large footed compote, crimpt. **410.** 72-5 Strawberry and Currant crimpt footed compote. **411.** 77-35 Sawtooth goblet. **412.** 22-3 Daisy and Button square ash tray. **413.** 22-30 Daisy and Button goblet, T. P. Panel. **414.** 22-69 Daisy and Button wine, T. P. Panel. **415.** 67-5 Wildflower goblet. **416.** 77-105 Rose Sprig goblet. **417.** 77-36 Strawberry and Currant goblet. **418.** 67-12 Wildflower wine. **419.** 22-23 Daisy and Button cream. **420.** 22-24 Daisy and Button sugar (sold as 22-23-24 cream and sugar set). **421.** 22-17 Daisy and Button 4" covered compote. **422.** 22-50 Daisy and Button square sauce. **423.** 70-8 7" Hen on Nest. **424.** 22-8 Daisy and Button 5" four-toed bowl. **425.** 7- Cherry basket (made from oval bowl). **426.** Moon and Star flared wine (not in line). **427.** 44-42 Moon and Star wine. **428.** 44-22 Moon and Star goblet. **429.** 7-5 Cherry sugar. **430.** 7-4 Cherry cream.

page 108
Carnival glass was first marketed by the Wright firm in the 1970s. **431.** 805-3 purple Carnival 14" Grape and Fruit plate c. 1977. **432.** 5-2 purple Carnival Iris tumbler c. 1979. **433.** 5-1 purple Carnival Iris water pitcher c. 1979. **434.** 820-2 12" Peacock plate. **435.** 2-2 purple Carnival Dahlia tumbler c. 1977. **436.** 2-1 purple Carnival Dahlia pitcher c. 1977. **437.** 2-1 white carnival Dahlia pitcher c. 1977. **438.** 2-2 white carnival Dahlia tumbler c. 1977 (also made in crystal and in ice blue carnival). **439.** 1776-T purple Carnival God and Home tumbler. **440.** 1776-WP purple Carnival God and Home pitcher. **441.** 1776-WP ruby Carnival God and Home pitcher c. 1980 (the 1776-T ruby Carnival God and Home tumbler was also made). **442.** 77-125 purple Carnival Grape rose bowl c. 1980. **443.** 70-17 amethyst Carnival/milk glass head Turkey c. 1979. **444.** 23-1 marigold Pony crimped bowl. **445.** 23-1 [purple] carnival Pony crimped bowl c. 1976 (these were also made as 23-1 flat plates from the old Dugan mould). **446.** 12-2 purple Carnival Grape Vine Lattice tumbler. **447.** 905 purple Carnival Grape and Daisy tumbler c. 1977. **448.** 820-1 purple Carnival Peacock bowl crimpt. **449.** 9-2 purple Carnival Banded Grape tumbler c. 1978. **450.** 800-3 purple Carnival Rambler Rose tumbler c. 1977.

page 109
Wright began to market these Stork and Rushes items in 1975. **451.** marigold carnival covered sugar. **452.** marigold carnival cream. **453.** marigold carnival spooner. **454.** marigold carnival tumbler. **455.** marigold carnival pitcher. **456.** blue opaque sauce. **457.** blue opaque bowl.

page 110
Wright's amber, unless otherwise indicated. **458.** sample 84-1 "amberina" pitcher, thumbprint. **459.** 7-1 Cherry large footed fruit bowl. **460.** Panel Grape epergne vase. **461.** 84-1 amber pitcher, thumbprint. **462.** 77-19 Cabbage Leaf goblet, satin finish. **463.** sample 77-43 Thousand Eye goblet made into ivy bowl. **464.** 3-4 Beaded small footed ivy bowl. **465.** 33-6 Hobnail cruet. **466.** 33-1 Hobnail barber bottle. **467.** 33-1 Hobnail barber bottle, satin finish. **468.** 77-33 Princess Feather goblet. **469.** 77-27 Inverted Dot goblet. **470.** 60-6 Tree of Life three-toed sauce. **471.** 44-17 Moon and Star cruet. **472.** 95-1 round cruet, thumbprint. **473.** 70-11 Stove covered candy box. **474.** 70-6 Frog covered candy box. **475.** 88-10 vaseline opalescent barber bottle, ribbed. **476.** 88-10 green opalescent barber bottle, ribbed. **477.** sample 84-3 vaseline opal dot pitcher.

page 111

Wright's amethyst, unless otherwise indicated. **478.** 7- 16 Cherry 10" oval bowl. **479.** early Cherry square crimped bowl **480.** Moon and Star cruet. **481.** 85-9 milk pitcher, rib. **482.** epergne (large central straight cone and three smaller curved cones) with opal crest. **483.** 85-1 milk pitcher, thumbprint. **484.** 95-1 round cruet, thumbprint. **485.** 22-47 Daisy and Button salt or pepper shaker. **486.** Daisy and Button hat. **487.** 96-1 sugar shaker, thumbprint. **488.** Melon handled bon bon (not in line after 1962) **489.** 96-11 sugar shaker, swirl. **490.** 90-1 tall cream, thumbprint. **491.** 77-63 S toothpick. **492.** Daisy and Button cream. **493.** 22-63 Daisy and Button round toothpick. **494.** 77-35 Sawtooth goblet. **495.** 22-41 Daisy and Button 8" scalloped plate. **496.** 22-35 Daisy and Button handled nappy. **497.** 22-17 Daisy and Button 4" covered compote. **498.** 22-25 Daisy and Button cruet. **499.** 77-3 Leaf ash tray. **500.** 22-2 Daisy and Button Fan ash tray.

page 112

Wright's green, unless otherwise indicated. **501.** 44-18 Moon and Star decanter, satin finish. **502.** vase, thumbprint. **503.** 33-1 Hobnail barber bottle. **504.** Panel Grape epergne vase. **505.** early shape pitcher, thumbprint. **506.** 77-98 Ribbed Palm Leaf goblet. **507.** "turkey foot" vase. **508.** 77-22 Daisy and Cube goblet, Forest deep plate etching. **509.** 72-2 Daisy and Cube compote (made from goblet), Forest deep plate etching. **510.** 77-16 Embossed Rose Triangle fairy light. **511.** 77-12 S cruet. **512.** 95-1 round cruet, thumbprint. **513.** 77-80 Panel Sawtooth sherbet. **514.** 70-5 Flat Iron covered candy box. **515-516.** 59-4 Stipple Star covered sugar and 59-3 cream. **517.** rose bowl, thumbprint. **518.** finger bowl, thumbprint. **519.** 77-46 Ferdinand mustard jar. **520.** green opalescent finger bowl, fern. **521.** ice tea, thumbprint.

page 113

522. green 77-79 Mirror and Rose goblet. **523.** pink 77-79 Mirror and Rose goblet. **524.** ruby Mirror and Rose pickle jar. **525.** amber Mirror and Rose pickle jar. **526.** pink 77-79 Mirror and Rose goblet (floral decoration). **527.** ruby 77-79 Mirror and Rose goblet (floral decoration). **528.** 7-15 caramel slag Cherry ice tea c. 1982. **529.** 7-14 caramel slag Cherry water pitcher c. 1982. **530-531.** green 77-107 Mirror and Rose salt and pepper shakers. **532.** green Mirror and Rose wine (floral decoration). **533.** amber Mirror and Rose wine (floral decoration). **534.** green Mirror and Rose wine. **535.** 77-22 black Daisy and Cube goblet, Forest etching. **536.** 77-21 purple slag Daisy and Cube goblet. **537.** 7-17 purple slag Cherry 5" oval bowl. **538.** 77-96 purple slag Trough. **539.** 77-95 purple slag Pump. **540.** 70-8 7" purple slag Hen on Nest. **541.** whimsey made from purple slag 77-35 Sawtooth goblet. **542.** 7-3 purple slag Cherry Scroll compote. **543.** purple slag 72-3 Dolphin compote.

page 114

544. 22-56 green Large Sleigh. **545.** 77-1 cobalt blue Colonial Carriage ash tray. **546.** 22-56 pink Large Sleigh. **547.** 22-54 Small Sleigh. **548.** 22-1 amethyst medium four wheel Cart ash tray. **549.** 22-1 blue Cart ash tray. **550.** Daisy and Button large four-wheel cart (not in line after 1962; Wright sometimes called this "Cinderella's cart"). **551.** 77-9 Three-Wheel Cart. **552** and **554.** Daisy and Button small four wheeled cart. **553.** 77-1 pink Colonial Carriage ash tray. **555.** 77-9 chocolate Three-Wheel Cart. **556.** 22-54 Small Sleigh. **557.** 22-55 Small Sleigh w/candleholder. **558.** 22-54 Small Sleigh.

page 115

559. amethyst epergne (large central straight cone and three smaller curved cones) with milk glass crest. **560.** Milk glass lamp with Moon and Star shade. **561.** Milk glass epergne large central straight cone and three smaller curved cones) with amethyst glass crest. **562.** amber 77-14 Grape decanter. **563.** amber Grape vase (satin finish). **564.** amethyst 77-14 Grape decanter. **565.** amber Grape vase **566.** amber 77-14 Grape decanter (satin finish).

pages 116-117

All of these Wright cranberry electric lamps **(567-582)** are the Thumbprint motif, but many combinations among lamp shades (ball shade, crimped shade or half shade), lamp fonts (round or pear-shaped) and lamp breaks are possible. Note that several of these have a milk glass base while others employ a brass base.

pages 118-119
From its introduction in the late 1940s, Wright's "amberina" remained a popular color, although relatively few pieces were in the line after the 1970s. **583.** 75-3 Petticoat vase. **584.** 44-19 Moon and star small epergne. **585.** Daisy and Cube toy lamp. **586.** Daisy and Button pickle caster. **587.** 22-20 Daisy and Button 6" round compote. **588.** 22-36 Daisy and Button pickle jar. **589.** 72-3 Dolphin compote. **590.** 7-4 Cherry cream. **591.** 7-5 Cherry sugar. **592.** 70-8 7" Hen on Nest. **593.** 22-7 Daisy and Button 10" four-toed bowl. **594.** 22-8 Daisy and Button 5" four-toed bowl. **595.** 22-28 Daisy and Button flower bowl w/block. **596.** 22-44 Daisy and Button rose bowl. **597.** 22-69 Daisy and Button T. P. Panel wine. **598.** 22-30 Daisy and Button T. P. Panel goblet. **599.** Daisy and Cube goblet. **600.** 22-54 Daisy and Button honey dish and cover. **601.** 7-1 Cherry large footed bowl. **602.** 33-2 Hobnail covered bowl. **603.** 33-7 Hobnail finger bowl. **604.** 33-9 Hobnail rose bowl. **605.** 22-3 Daisy and Button square ash tray. **606.** Daisy and Button bone tray. **607.** 22-5 Daisy and Button 6" crimped bowl. **608.** 7-2 Cherry butter and cover.**609.** 22-16 Daisy and Button canoe. **610.** 22-50 Daisy and Button square sauce. **611.** 77-53 Thistle salt dip. **612.** 44-3 Moon and Star 9" candlesticks. **613.** 44-5 Moon and Star 11" console bowl. **614.** 22-10 Daisy and Button large Shell footed bowl. **615.** 44-1 Moon and Star large ash tray. **616.** 44-4 Moon and Star 6" candlesticks. **617.** 44-6 Moon and Star 8" console bowl. **618.** 22-63 Daisy and Button toothpick. **619.** 77-50 Bird salt dip. **620.** 22-12 Daisy and Button oval butter and cover. **621-622.** Daisy and Button 22-23 sugar and 22-24 cream.

page 120
623-626. amethyst, amber, blue and green 22-5 Daisy and Button 6" crimpt bowl. **627-628.** blue and amber 77-75 Hoot Owl relish dishes. **629-631.** amber, blue and amethyst 22-50 Daisy and Button 4" square sauces. **632-633.** amber and blue 22-27 Daisy and Button finger bowl. **634-635.** amber and blue 22-57 Daisy and Button Kitten slippers. **636-638.** amethyst, amber and blue 77-1 Colonial Carriage ash tray. **639-642.** amber, green, blue and amethyst 77-3 Leaf ash trays. **643-645.** amber, blue and amethyst 22-32 Daisy and Button medium hats. **646-650.** amberina, blue, amber, amethyst and green 22-63 Daisy and Button round toothpicks. **651-655.** amethyst, ruby, blue, green and amber 22-58 Daisy and Button medium slippers. **656-658.** blue, amethyst and amber 22-33 Daisy and Button small hats. **659-662.** amberina, amethyst, blue and amber 77-50 Bird salt dips. **663-666.** amethyst, amber, blue and green 22-2 Daisy and Button small fan ash trays. **667-670.** green, blue, amethyst and amber 22-45 Daisy and Button round salt dips. **671-675.** green, amber, ruby, blue and amethyst 11-8 Double Wedding Ring salt dips. **676-679.** blue, green amber and amethyst 22-59 Daisy and Button small slippers.

page 121
680-684. 59-6 Stipple Star goblets in ruby, blue, amethyst, amber and green. **685.** 66-3 crystal Westward Ho goblet. **686-688.** 77-24 Grasshopper goblets in blue, amethyst and amber. **689-692.** 67-4 Wildflower sugar and cover and 67-3 Wildflower cream in amber and blue. **693-694.** 77-35 Sawtooth goblets in ruby and dark blue. **695-697.** 77-30 Morning Glory goblets in amber, ruby and blue. **698-705.** 55-5 Panel Grape cream and sugar sets in blue, amethyst, amber and green. **706-708.** 77-72 Coal Hod ash trays in amber, blue and green. **709-713.** 77-77 Sawtooth wines in dark blue, ruby, blue, green and amber. **714-717.** 65-7 Three Face salt and pepper shakers in blue (satin finish) and amber (satin finish). **718.** 65-9 Three Face toothpick in camphor/satin finish. **719.** 65-6 Three Face salt dip in camphor/satin finish. **720-723.** 55-20 Panel Grape wines in amethyst, amber, green and blue.

page 122
724-725. 59-2 Stipple Star 6" covered compotes in blue and amber. **726-727.** 59-1 Stipple Star 8" covered compotes in blue and amber. **728-730.** 67-10 Wildflower stick candy jars in blue, crystal and

amber. **731-742.** 59-4 Stipple Star sugar and cover and 59-3 Stipple Star cream in ruby, crystal, blue, amethyst, amber and green. **743-745.** 77-45 Strawberry and Currant mugs in amethyst, blue and amber. **746-751.** 59-7 Stipple Star wines in amethyst, amber, ruby, blue, crystal and green. **752-756.** 77-68 Strawberry and Currant wines in crystal, blue, amber, green and ruby. **757-762.** 59-5 Stipple star salt dips in amber, green, ruby, crystal, blue and amethyst. **763-765.** 22-35 Daisy and Button 6¹/₂" handled nappys in amber, amethyst and blue.

page 123

766-769. 77-12 S cruets in green, blue, ruby and amber. **770-771.** 33-6 Hobnail cruets in blue and amber (note different stoppers). **772-774.** 22-35 Daisy and Button cruets in amethyst, amber and blue. **775-782.** 7-5 Cherry sugar and 7-4 Cherry cream in blue, green, ruby and amber. **783-785.** 33-10 Hobnail salt/pepper shakers in blue, amethyst and amber. **786-790.** 77-65 Tree Stump toothpicks in blue, ruby, amber, amethyst and green. **791-796.** 7-8 Cherry toothpicks in ruby, green, amber, blue amethyst and amberina. **797-801.** 77-52 Swan salt dips in green, pink, amber, blue and amethyst. **802-806.** 22-47 Daisy and Button salt/pepper shakers in blue, pink, green, amber and amethyst. **807-811.** 44-39 Moon and Star toothpicks in green, amber, amethyst, blue and ruby. **812-816.** 77-53 Thistle salt dips in amethyst, blue, amber, amberina and green.

page 124

817, 819 and **821.** 77-9 3-wheel Carts in blue, amethyst and amber. **818** and **820.** 7-10 Cherry pitchers in amber and blue. **822-823** and **825-826.** 70-5 Flat Iron candy boxes in green, blue, amber and amethyst. **824.** vaseline opalescent 22-11 Daisy and Button 11" star-shaped berry berry bowl. **827-828.** 70-6 Frog candy boxes. **829-833.** 3-4 Beaded small footed ivy bowls in blue, amethyst, vaseline opalescent, blue opalescent and amber. **834-841.** 77-11 Sweetheart sugar and cream sets in blue, ruby, crystal and amber.

page 125

842-844. Acorn Squirrel covered candy boxes in amber, milk glass and blue. **845-847.** 22-19 Daisy and Button large square covered compotes in amber, crystal and blue. **848-849.** 35-4 Jersey Swirl footed compotes in amber and blue. **850-851.** 35-5 Jersey Swirl goblets in blue and amber. **852-854.** 22-18 Daisy and Button 6" oval covered compotes in crystal, blue and amber. **855.** ruby 77-37 Sweetheart goblet. **856.** crystal 77-42 101 Ranch goblet. **857.** crystal 77-26 Horn of Plenty goblet. **858-859.** ruby 77-11 Sweetheart cream and sugar set. **860.** amber Sweetheart sugar. **861.** amber 77-27 Inverted Dot goblet. **862-863.** Diamond Panel Fruits goblets in amber and blue. **864.** 77-36 Strawberry and Current goblet in dark amethyst. **865.** 77-21 Daisy and Cube goblet in dark amethyst. **866.** crystal 44-31 Moon and Star salt shaker. **867-869.** Crystal, amber and blue 22-31 Daisy and Button Gypsy Kettle w/cover and spoon. **870-872.** 77-63 S toothpicks in crystal, blue and amber. **873.** amber 22-45 Daisy and Button round salt dip. **874.** dark green 22-67 Daisy and Button tumbler. **875.** amethyst 33-7 Hobnail finger bowl, crimpt.

page 126

876-878. This stemware (goblet, sherbet and wine) with cranberry bowls and crystal stem/foot was made by Salvatore "Sam" Diana's Venetian Glass Co. and was in the Wright line for a brief period in the 1950s. **889-893.** 59-6 Stipple Star goblets in blue, crystal, green, amber and amethyst. **894-895.** Morning Glory 77-30 goblet and 77-67 wine. **896-898.** 64-7 Thistle wines in blue, crystal and amber. **899.** crystal 44-17 Moon and Star cruet with stopper. **900-903.** 77-24 Grasshopper goblets in amber, crystal, blue and green. **904-905** and **909-910.** Melon handled bon bons in green, blue, amethyst and amber. **906-908.** 64-32 Thistle stemmed sherbets in amber, blue and crystal. **911-914.** 77-48 Crescent Planter in blue, amber, green and amethyst.

page 127

915-916. 22-39 Daisy and Button 10" plates in blue and amber. **917-918.** 22-37 Daisy and Button water pitchers in blue and amber. **919-921.** 22-21 Daisy and Button large creams in blue, amber and green.

922- 923. 22-36 Daisy and Button pickle jar w/metal cover in amber and blue. **924-926.** 22-70 Daisy and Button bell candy boxes in amber, green and blue. **927-928.** 22-65 Daisy and Button large fan trays in amber and blue. **929-933.** 22-17 Daisy and Button 4" covered compotes in amberina, amber, amethyst, green and blue. **934-935.** 22-67 Daisy and Button tumblers in amber and blue. **936-939.** 22-44 Daisy and Button rose bowls in amber, blue, green and amethyst. **940-943.** 22-24 Daisy and Button small sugar and 22-23 Daisy and Button small cream in amber and blue. **944-945.** 22-52 Daisy and Button square footed sherbets in amber and blue. **946.** 22-28 amber Daisy and Button flower bowl w/crystal block. **947-948.** 22-12 Daisy and Button oval butter and cover in blue and amber.

page 128
949-952 and **955.** 22-11 Daisy and Button 11" star berry bowls in green, blue, amber, amethyst and amberina. **953-954.** Daisy and Button cheese dishes in amber and blue. **956-959.** 22-4 Daisy and Button baskets in amethyst, amber, green and blue. **960-963.** 22-15 Daisy and Button stove candleholder in blue, green, amber and amethyst. **964-968.** 22-51 Daisy and Button 5" star sauce dishes in amberina, amethyst, green, blue and amber. **969-972.** Daisy and Button boat ash trays in green, blue, amethyst and amber. **973-976.** Daisy and Button wall planters in blue, amber, amethyst and green (these are flat on one side and have holes at each end). **977-980.** 22-46 Daisy and Button triangle salt dips in amber, amethyst, blue and green.

page 129
This array of pink glassware was probably made for Wright by the Fostoria Glass Co. **981.** 44-33 Moon and Star 10" salver. **982.** 44-22 Moon and Star goblet. **983.** 44-14 Moon and Star 8" open compote. **984.** 77-35 Sawtooth goblet. **985.** 77-31 Panel Daisy goblet. **986.** 44-11 Moon and Star 8" covered compote. **987.** 22-20 Daisy and Button 6" round covered compote. **988.** 22-17 Daisy and Button 4" covered compote. **989.** 22-12 Daisy and Button oval butter and cover. **990.** 22-30 Daisy and Button goblet with Thumbprint panel. **991.** 22-69 Daisy and Button wine with Thumbprint panel. **992.** 22-24 Daisy and Button small square sugar. **993.** 22-23 Daisy and Button small square cream. **994.** 22-35 Daisy and Button handled nappy. **995.** 22-40 Daisy and Button 7" round scalloped plate. **996.** 22-39 Daisy and Button 10" plate. **997.** 44-42 Moon and Star wine. **998.** 22-53 Daisy and Button square footed sherbet.

page 130
Moon and Star items. **999-1003.** 44-8 4" covered compotes in amethyst, blue, green, amber and ruby. **1004-1007** and **1010.** 44-25 footed juice glasses in green, amethyst, blue, ruby and amber. **1008, 1011, 1013, 1015** and **1017.** 44-26 8' plates in ruby, amber, green, amethyst and blue. **1009, 1012, 1014, 1016** and **1018.** 44-36 high footed sherbets in ruby, amber, green, amethyst and blue. **1019-1023.** 44-27 handled relish dishes in amber, green, blue, pink and amethyst. **1024-1028.** 44-8" rectangular relish dishes in amethyst, amber, blue and green.

page 131
1028-1031. 44-47 6" stemmed covered candy boxes in blue, amber, ruby and green. **1032-1033** and **1038-1039.** 77-74 S plates in ruby, amber, blue and green. **1034-1037.** 44-48 7" stemmed open compotes (flared) in ruby, blue, green and amber. **1040-1043.** 44-50 4¹/₂" stemmed covered jellies covered compotes in amber, ruby, blue and green. **1044-1045** and **1050-1051.** 77-76 S sherbets in ruby, amber, green and blue. **1046-1049.** 44-49 5" stemmed open compotes (flared) in green, amber, ruby and blue.

page 132
1052-1057. 44-1 Moon and Star ash trays in blue, amber, ruby, amethyst, green and amberina. **1058.** 44-37 amber Moon and Star spooner. **1059.** 44-38 amber Moon and Star large sugar and cover. **1060.** 44-16 amber Moon and Star large cream. **1061.** 44-52 amber Moon and Star low sugar and cover. **1062.** 44-2 amber Moon and Star butter and cover. **1063-1066.** 44-41 Moon and Star tumblers in ruby, amber, green and blue. **1067.** 44-43 ruby Moon and Star nappy, flared (also made crimpt). **1068.** 44-44 ruby

Moon and Star rose bowl. **1069.** 44-45 ruby Moon and Star flower bowl w/block. **1070-1071.** 44-52 Moon and Star low sugar and cover in ruby and blue. **1072-1073.** 44-7 Moon and Star champagnes in amber and ruby. **1074-1076.** 44-17 Moon and Star cruet in blue, amber and amethyst. **1077-1079.** 44-21 Moon and Star finger bowls in blue, amber and green. **1080-1083.** 44-25 Moon and Star juice glasses in ruby, green, amber and blue. **1084-1085.** 44-35 Moon and Star footed sauces in ruby and amber.

page 133

1086-1092. Acorn covered candy boxes in amethyst, amber (satin finished), blue (satin finished), milk, blue, amber and green. **1093-1096.** 22-17 Daisy and Button 4" covered compotes in green, blue, amber and amethyst. **1097.** amber Daisy and Button mustard with wire handle. **1098-1101.** 77-54 Embossed Rose salt/pepper shakers in crystal, blue, amber and amethyst. **1102-1106.** 77-60 Frog toothpicks in amber, milk, amethyst, green and blue. **1107-1112.** 77-129 Chick Basket toothpick holders in crystal, blue, green, amethyst, milk and amber. **1113-1115.** 22-1 Daisy and Button small cart ash trays in amethyst, amber and blue. **1116-1120.** Daisy and Button Anvil ash trays in milk, green, amethyst, blue and amber. **1121-1124** and **1129.** 77-1 Colonial Carriage ash trays in green, milk, blue, amethyst and pink. **1125-1128.** 77-3 Leaf ash trays in blue, amethyst, amber and green. **1130.** 22-1 Daisy and Button small four wheeled cart ash tray in green. **1131-1135.** Daisy and Button Sandles in milk glass, blue, amethyst, green and amber.

pages 134-135

Ruby was a popular color in the Wright line, and many of these pieces were made for Wright at the Viking Glass Co. in New Martinsville. **1136.** 77-26 Horn of Plenty goblet. **1137-1138.** Panel Grape 55-7 goblet and 55-9 pitcher. **1139.** 44-18 Moon and Star decanter. **1140.** 77-21Daisy and Cube goblet. **1150.** 44- Moon and Star goblet **1151.** 77-25 Herringbone goblet. **1152.** 33-8 Hobnail goblet. **1153.** 22-30 Daisy and Button goblet with Thumbprint panel. **1154.** 35-5 Jersey Swirl goblet. **1155.** 77-36 Strawberry and Currant goblet. **1156.** 59-6 Stipple Star goblet. **1157.** 77-23 Diamond Quilted goblet. **1158.** 77-37 Sweetheart goblet. **1159.** 77-63 S toothpick. **1160-1161.** 33-10 Hobnail salt and pepper shakers. **1162.** 55-20 Panel Grape wine. **1163.** 77-66 Diamond Quilted wine. **1164.** 22-69 Daisy and Button wine with Thumbprint panel. 1165. 45-42 Moon and Star wine. **1166-1167.** 45-31 Moon and Star salt and pepper shakers. **1168.** 45-39 Moon and Star toothpick. **1169.** 45-30 Moon and Star salt dip. **1170.** 22-45 Daisy and Button round salt dip. **1171.** 22-46 Daisy and Button triangular salt dip. These Panel Grape items in ruby were in the Wright line throughout most of the 1960s. **1172.** 55-16 4" sauce. **1173-1174.** 55-5 cream and sugar set. **1175.** 55-7 goblet. **1176.** 55-8 covered jelly compote. **1177.** 55-18 sherbet. **1178.** 55-20 wine. **1179-1180.** 5-6 cup and 55-17 Panel Grape saucer. **1181.** 55-11 10" plate. **1182.** 55-10 15" plate. **1183.** 55-12 8" plate. **1184.** 55-9 water pitcher. **1185.** 55-2 lily bowl. **1186.** 55-14 P15 pc. punch set (12 cups, bowl, ladle and underplate). **1187.** 55-6 punch cup. **1188.** 55-1 console bowl, crimpt.

pages 136-137

Vaseline opalescent items. **1189.** fluted barber bottle, rib. **1190.** fluted barber bottle, fern (satin finished). **1191.** tumbler, fern (satin finished). **1192.** pitcher, fern **1193.** tumbler, fern. **1194.** cruet, fern. **1195.** round cruet, fern. **1196.** 3-4 Beaded small footed ivy ball. **1197.** 72-5 Strawberry and Currant compote. **1198.** 22-7 Daisy and Button 10" oval bowl. **1199.** 77-121 (also 75-1) Corn vase. **1200.** 35-4 Jersey Swirl footed compote, crimpt. **1201.** 22-63 Daisy and Button round toothpick. **1202.** 22-50 Daisy and Button 4" square sauce. **1203.** 22-8 Daisy and Button 5" oval bowl. **1204.** 22-17 Daisy and Button 4" round covered compote. **1205.** 72-3 Dolphin compote. **1206.** 3-3 Beaded large footed bowl, crimpt. **1207.** 70-8 7" Hen (satin finish). **1208.** 70-8 7" Hen. **1209.** 22-19 Daisy and Button 6" square covered compote. **1210.** 22-39 Daisy and Button 10" plate. **1211.** Daisy and Button square plate. **1212.** 44-22 Moon and Star goblet. **1213.** Wildflower goblet. **1214.** 22-30 Daisy and Button goblet with Thumbprint panel. **1215.** 67-1 Wildflower 6" covered compote.**1216.** 77-36 Strawberry and Currant goblet. **1217.** 35-5 Jersey Swirl goblet. **1218.** 22-3 Daisy and Button 6" square ashtray. **1219.** 44-22 Moon and star wine. **1220.** 67-12 Wildflower wine. **1221.** 22-69 Daisy and Button wine with

Thumbprint panel. **1222-1223.** 7-5 Cherry sugar and 7-4 cream. **1224-1225.** 22-24 Daisy and Button square sugar and 22-23 cream.

page 138
1226 and **1230.** Daisy and Button fan vases in amber and blue. **1227** and **1229.** Moon and Star vases in blue and amber. **1228, 1233, 1237, 1239** and **1242.** 3-5 Beaded large ivy bowl in ruby, amber, blue, green and amethyst. **1231, 1235, 1236, 1240** and **1241.** 3-3 Beaded 8" large crimpt bowl in amber, ruby, amethyst, blue and green. **1232, 1234, 1238** and **1243.** 3-3 Beaded 8" large flared bowl in ruby, blue, green and amber.

page 139
1244-1247. 22-41 Daisy and Button 8" scalloped plates in amethyst, amber, blue and amberina. **1248-1251.** 77-35 Sawtooth goblets in amber, green, blue and amethyst. **1252-1254.** 77-47 Embossed Rose triangle nappys in green, amber and blue. **1255-1258.** 22-53 daisy and Button skillets in amber, amberina, amethyst and blue. **1259-1261.** 70-11 Stove covered candy boxes in amethyst, blue and amber. **1262-1264.** 70-16 Embossed Rose triangle fairy lamps in blue, green (satin finished) and amber. **1265-1267.** Horse Shoe ash trays in green, amethyst and amber. **1268-1270.** Horse Shoe covered candy boxes in green, amber and amethyst.

page 140
1271-1274. 70-7 3" Hen on Nest in amethyst, amberina, blue and amber. **1275-1279.** 77-8 Bee Hive honey dishes in amberina, amber, blue, green and amethyst. **1280-1285.** 22-64 Daisy and Button triangle toothpicks in amethyst, amber, ruby, blue, green and amberina. **1286-1291.** 77-10 Daisy and Cube sugar and cream sets in amber, blue and green. **1292-1295.** 77-64 Sweetheart toothpicks in ruby, amethyst, green and amber. **1296-1300.** 77-61 Rabbit toothpicks in amethyst, green, amberina, amber and blue. **1301-1304.** 77-59 Fish toothpicks in amberina, blue, amber and amethyst. **1305-1308.** 77-62 Rooster toothpicks in blue, green, amethyst and amber. **1309-1313.** 7-6 Cherry rectangular salt dip in amethyst, amberina, blue, amber and green. **1314-1315.** 77-51 Frog salt dips in amber and green. **1316-1319.** 77-2 Fish ash tray in green, amethyst, amber and blue. **1320-1324.** 77-6 Violin ash trays in ruby, amber, amethyst, green and blue.

page 141
These Wright animals, marketed as covered candy boxes, were quite popular in the mid-1960s. Except for the Rabbit and the Duck, all use the same basketweave-style base. **1325-1327.** 80-11 5" Rabbit in blue, amber and amethyst. **1328-1330.** 80-5 5" Duck in blue , amber and amberina. **1331-1333.** 80-3 5" Cow in amber, amethyst and blue. **1334-1338.** 80-16 5" Turtle in green, amethyst, blue, amberina and amber. **1339-1340.** 80-10 5" Owl in blue and amber. **1341-1345.** 80-12 5" Rooster in green, amethyst, blue, amber and amberina. **1346-1348.** 80-6 5" frog in blue, amber and green. **1349-1353.** 80-7 5" Hen in amber, green, amberina, blue and amethyst. **1354-1356.** 80-1 5" Bird in amber, blue and amberina. **1357-1359.** 80-14 5" Swan in amethyst, blue and amber. **1360-1361.** 80-8 5" Horse in blue and amber. **1362-1363.** 80-9 5" Lamb in blue and amber. **1364-1367.** 80-15 5" Turkey in blue, amber, amberina and amethyst.

pages 142-143
Purple Slag items. **1368.** 77-63 S toothpick. **1369.** 77-8 Beehive. **1370.** 70-18 3" Hen. **1371.** 70-8 7" Hen. **1372.** 70-2 Atterbury Duck. **1373.** 7-3 Cherry 6" open compote. **1374.** 77-59 Fish toothpick. **1375.** 77-35 Sawtooth goblet. **1376-1377.** 7-4 Cherry cream and 7-5sugar. **1378.** 22-3 Daisy and Button 6" square ash tray. **1379.** 80-16 Turtle. **1380.** 80-6 Frog. **1381.** Daisy and Button fan vase. **1382.** 77-46 Ferdinand mustard jar. **1383.** 80-11 Rabbit. **1384.** 80-12 Rooster. **1385.** 80-14 Swan. **1386.** 80-15 Turkey. **1387.** 80-7 Hen. **1388.** 80-8 Horse. **1389.** 80-9 Lamb. **1390.** 80-3 Cow. **1391.** 80-1 Bird. **1392-1394.** 80-5 Duck. **1395.** 80-10 Owl.

page 144

These animal covered dishes in dark blue or dark blue with satin finish were in the Wright line throughout most of the 1960s. Except for the Rabbit, all of the 5" animals use the same basketweave-style base. **1396.** 80-7 5" Hen (satin finish). **1397.** 80-12 5" Rooster (satin finish). **1398.** 70-8 7" Hen on Nest (satin finish). **1399.** 70-8 7" Hen on Nest. **1400.** 80-7 5" Hen. **1401.** 80-14 5" Swan (satin finish). **1402.** 80-16 5" Turtle (satin finish). **1403.** 80-10 5" Owl (satin finish). **1404.** 80-10 5" Owl. **1405.** 80-12 5" Rooster. **1406.** 80-1 5" Bird (satin finish). **1407.** 80-7 5" Hen. **1408.** 80-8 5" Horse. **1409.** 80-9 5" Lamb. **1410.** 80-3 5" Cow. **1411.** 80-1 5" Bird. **1412.** 80-6 5" Frog. **1413.** 80-16 5" Turtle. **1414.** 80-14 5" Swan. **1415.** 80-11 5" Rabbit.

page 145

The Panel Grape pieces shown on this page were made from the same mould. **1416, 1422,** and **1426-1428.** 55-3 Panel Grape covered compote in green, amber, ruby, blue and amethyst. **1417-1421.** 22-61 Daisy and Button stick candy jar in blue, green, ruby, amber and amethyst. **1423-1425** and **1431.** 55-4 Panel Grape 8" open compote in amethyst, amber, blue and ruby. **1429-1430, 1432-1433** and **1436.** 55-15 Panel Grape salver in amber, blue, amethyst, ruby and green. **1434-1435** and **1437-1438.** 70-14 Violin covered candy boxes in amethyst, amber, blue and green.

page 146

1439-1441. 75-1 Corn vases in blue opalescent, amber and blue. **1442-1445.** 35-2 Jersey Swirl 5" d. high footed covered compotes in green, amber, amberina and blue. **1446-1448.** 75-3 Petticoat vases in amber, green and blue. **1449-1452.** 35-3 Jersey Swirl 5" d. low footed covered compotes in amber, amberina, blue and green. **1453-1455.** 72-3 Dolphin compotes in amber, blue and amethyst. **1456-1458.** 5-2 Beaded Grape cruets in amber, blue and green. **1459.** 5-1 green Beaded Grape square covered compote. **1460.** 5-4 green Beaded Grape 8" square plate. **1461-1463.** 5-3 Beaded Grape goblets in green, ruby and amber. **1464.** 35-5 amber Jersey Swirl goblet. **1465-1468.** 35-4 Jersey Swirl crimpt compotes in amber, ruby, green and blue (made from goblet).

page 147

1469-1473. 11-1 Double Wedding Ring 6" covered compotes in green, blue, ruby, amber and amethyst. **1474-1478.** 11-3 Double Wedding Ring 4" covered jelly compotes in blue, ruby, amber, amethyst and green. **1479-1483.** 11-6 Double Wedding Ring toothpicks in blue, amethyst, ruby, green and amber. **1484-1488.** 11-7 Double Wedding Ring wines in green, amber, ruby, blue and amethyst. **1489, 1491, 1493, 1495** and **1497.** 11-4 Double Wedding Ring 8" plates in ruby, blue, amethyst, green and amber. **1490, 1492, 1494, 1496** and **1498.** 11-5 Double Wedding Ring sherbets in ruby, blue, amethyst, green and amber.

page 148

1499-1500 and **1502-1504.** 77-41 Wildrose goblets in amethyst, ruby, blue, green and amber. **1501** and **1510-1511.** 72-6 Wildrose footed compotes in amber, ruby and amethyst (made from goblet). **1505-1509.** 77-69 Wildrose wines in green, amethyst, blue, ruby and amber. **1512, 1514** and **1516.** 77-23 Princess Feather goblets in amber, blue and crystal. **1513, 1515** and **1517.** 77-57 Princess Feather tulip sundaes in amber, blue and crystal. **1518-1519.** 70-3 Embossed Rose four-toed covered candy box in blue, green and amber. **1521-1522.** 77-40 Wheat and Barley goblets in blue and amber.

page 149

1523-1527. 77-34 S goblets in green, amber, ruby, blue and amethyst. **1528-1532.** 77-71 S wines in amber, amethyst, ruby, blue and green. **1533-1534** and **1539-1540.** 56-1 Priscilla 4" covered jelly compotes in crystal, ruby, green and amber. **1535-1538.** 56-2 Priscilla goblets in amber, crystal, green and ruby. **1541-1543.** 56-3 Priscilla round sauce dishes in green, crystal and amber. **1544-1549.** 56-4 Priscilla toothpicks in green, ruby, blue, amethyst and amber.

page 150

1550-1554. 56-5 Priscilla ash trays in blue, ruby, crystal, green and amber. **1555-1558.** 56-7 Priscilla 8" plates in ruby, blue, green and amber. **1559** and **1565-1567.** 56-6 Priscilla 6¹/₂" crimpt nappys in ruby, amber, green and crystal. **1560-1564.** 56-8 Priscilla rose bowls in green, blue, ruby, amber and crystal. **1568-1572.** 56-10 Priscilla wines in blue, ruby, crystal, amber and green. **1573-1577.** 56-9 Priscilla sherbets in amber, crystal, green, ruby and blue.

page 151

1578-1581. 25-1 Eye-Winker 6" covered compotes in green, amber, ruby and blue. **1582-1586.** 25-3 Eye-Winker goblets in ruby, crystal, amber, green and blue. **1587-1590.** 25-2 Eye-winker 7¹/₂" open compotes in blue, ruby, amber and green (made from base to 25-1 covered compote). **1591-1594.** 25-4 Eye-Winker sherbets in amber, green, blue and ruby. **1595-1597.** 77-78 Wildrose nappys in amber, blue and green. **1598-1601.** 77-73 Wildrose ice teas in ruby, blue, amber and green. **1602-1605.** 25-7 Eye-Winker wines in green, blue, ruby and amber. **1606-1609.** 25-5 Eye-winker sauce dishes in blue, amber, green and ruby (the ruby is hand-finished with a slightly flared rim).

page 152

1610-1612. 25-10 Eye-Winker 10" footed bowls in amber, ruby and green. **1613-1615.** 25-15 Eye-Winker 5" low footed covered compotes in ruby, amber and green. **1616-1618.** 25-16 Eye-Winker 6" high footed compotes in green, amber and ruby. **1619-1621.** 25-17 Eye-Winker 5" low footed open compotes in green, ruby and amber (made from 25-15 low footed compote base). **1622-1624.** 25-20 Eye-Winker honey dishes in amber, ruby and green. **1625-1627.** 25-12 Eye-Winker butter and cover in amber, ruby and green. **1628-1629.** 25-21 Eye-Winker pickle trays in green and amber. **1630-1631.** 25-11 Eye-Winker 5" four-toed bowls in green and amber. **1632** and **1634.** 25-14 Eye-Winker 4" covered compotes in green and ruby. **1633** and **1635.** 25-4 Eye-Winker sherbets in amber and blue (this item is the base for the 25-14 covered compote). **1636-1638.** 25-9 Eye-Winker 4¹/₂" ash trays in green, amber and ruby. **1639, 1641** and **1643.** 25-19 Eye-Winker sugar and cover in green, ruby and amber. **1640, 1642** and **1644.** 25-18 Eye-Winker cream in green, ruby and amber.

page 153

1645-1648. 25-27 Eye-Winker tumblers in blue, amber, ruby and green. **1649-1652.** 25-25 Eye-Winker covered marmalades in blue, amber, green and amber. **1653-1656.** 25-28 Eye-Winker 6" vases in amber, ruby, green and blue. **1657-1660.** 25-26 Eye-Winker pitchers in green, amber, blue and ruby. **1661-1665.** 77-90 Grape 10" oval bowls in blue, amberina, amethyst, green and amber. **1666-1670.** 77-89 Wildrose ash tray sets in amethyst, amber, blue, ruby and green (each set consists of 77-86 7" Wildrose ash tray, 77-87 6" Wildrose ash tray, and 77-88 Wildrose 4" ash tray).

page 154

1671-1673. 56-11 Priscilla covered compotes in amber, ruby and green. **1674-1676.** 56-12 Priscilla 7" open compotes in amber, ruby and green. **1677-1680.** 77-79 Mirror and Rose goblets in green, amber, pink and ruby. **1681-1682.** 77-85 Mirror and Rose wines in green and pink. **1683-1684.** 77-82 Sweetheart wines in amber and ruby. **1685-1688.** 77-81 Daisy and Cube wines in amber, ruby, green and amberina. **1689-1691.** 77-80 Sawtooth sherbets in amber, ruby and green. **1692-1694.** 22-72 Daisy and Button 7" Shell footed bowls in amberina, green and amber. **1695.** 44-54 green Moon and Star sugar shaker. **1696-1700.** 44-53 Moon and Star 5" ash trays in amberina, pink, green, ruby and amber. **1701-1702.** 25-8 Eye-Winker 7" ash trays in green and amber. **1703-1705.** 25-23 Eye-Winker toothpicks in green, ruby and amber. **1706-1708.** 25-22 Eye-Winker salt dips in ruby, green and amber. **1709-1716.** 25-24 Eye-Winker salt/pepper shakers in green, amber, crystal and ruby.

page 155

1717-1719. 77-37 Sweetheart goblets in blue, amber and ruby. **1720-1722.** 77-19 Cabbage Leaf goblets in blue, crystal and amber (all satin finished). **1723-1725.** 67-5 Wildflower goblets in blue, ruby and amber. **1726-1729.** 35-5 Jersey Swirl goblets in green, ruby, blue and amber. **1730-1731.** 77-22 Daisy and Cube goblets with Forest etching. **1732-1736.** 77-21 Daisy and Cube goblets in amberina, green, blue, ruby and amber. **1737-1741.** 77-23 Diamond Quilted goblets in ruby, amethyst, green, blue and amber. **1742-1746.** 33-8 Hobnail goblets in ruby, amber, amethyst, green and blue. **1747-1751.** 37-2 Magnet and Grape goblets in amethyst, green, amber, blue and ruby. **1752-1756.** 77-36 Strawberry and Currant goblets in green, ruby, amber, amethyst and blue.

page 156

1757-1758. 77-43 Thousand Eye goblets in amber and blue. **1759-1760.** 22-29 Daisy and Button goblets (plain stem) in amber and blue. **1761.** amber 77-25 Inverted Dot goblet. **1762.** ruby 77-26 Horn of Plenty goblet. **1763.** amber 77-29 Maple Leaf goblet. **1764-1769.** 22-69 Daisy and Button wines (Thumbprint panel) in amberina, green, blue, ruby, amber and amethyst. **1770-1774.** 37-5 Magnet and Grape wines in blue, green, ruby, amber and amethyst. **1775-1779.** 55-20 Panel Grape goblets in ruby, amber, amethyst, blue and green. **1780-1782.** 67-12 Wildflower wines in ruby, amber and blue. **1783-1784.** 77-70 Cabbage Leaf wines in blue and amber (satin finished). **1785-1790.** 22-30 Daisy and Button goblets (Thumbprint panel) in amberina, blue, ruby, green, amber and amethyst. **1791-1793.** 77-25 Herringbone goblets in ruby, amber and green.

page 157

1794-1795. decorated Holland Rose and Rose of Yesteryear "slim vase" vases. **1796-1798.** 70-16 tall Wildrose covered compotes in amber, green and ruby. **1799-1801.** 10", 8" and 6" apothecary jars (decorated Holland Rose). **1802, 1805, 1809** and **1812.** Cranberry pickle casters in thumbprint, fern, swirl and dot motifs. **1803-1804** and **1806.** 40-8-5 Maize pickle jars in pink overlay, amber overlay and dark blue overlay. **1807, 1810** and **1811.** Daisy and Button pickle jars in amberina, blue and amber. **1813-1815.** 70-15 Embossed Rose 4" four-toed covered candy boxes in blue, green and amber. **1816-1817.** 77-94 Strawberry and Currant creams in green and amber. **1818** and **1820.** 77-96 Trough in green and amber. **1819** and **1821.** 77-95 Pump in green and amber. **1822-1825.** 77-92 Queen Anne slippers in amber, amethyst, green and blue (mould owned by Mosser). **1826-1830.** 77-93 Turkey toothpicks in amethyst, amber, blue and green (mould owned by Mosser). **1831-1834.** 25-29 Eye-Winker fairy lamps in blue, green, amber and ruby. **1835-1838.** 77-91 High Button Shoes in amethyst, green, blue and amber (mould owned by Mosser).

page 158

1839-1842. 75-4 Embossed Rose rose bowls in amber overlay, Peach Blow, rose overlay and light blue overlay. **1843-1851.** 40-2 Maize rose bowls in light blue overlay, cranberry, amber overlay (satin finish), cranberry (satin finish), Peach Blow, rose overlay, amber overlay, rose overlay (satin finish) and dark blue overlay.

page 159

Except for the Maize water pitcher and Maize lamp. these articles were available with either plain or satin finish. **1852.** 40-5 pink overlay Maize water pitcher. **1853.** 40-7 pink overlay Maize 9" vase. **1854.** 40-5 amber overlay Maize water pitcher. **1855.** 40-7 amber overlay Maize 9" vase. **1856-1857.** 40-4 Maize tumblers in amber overlay and pink overlay (satin finished). **1858-1859.** 40-3 Maize sugar shakers in amber overlay and pink overlay (satin finished). **1860-1861.** 40-6 Maize 7" vases in amber overlay and pink overlay (satin finished). **1862.** amber overlay Maize lamp. **1863.** 99-28 pink overlay Embossed Bird 13" vase. **1864.** 99-29 milk glass Embossed Bird 13" vase. **1865.** 99-27 amber overlay Embossed Bird 13" vase.

page 160

Toy lamps were an integral part of the Wright line for many years. **1866.** Cranberry 10-6 dot toy lamp with half shade. **1867-1868.** Cranberry eye dot toy lamps with half shade and ball shade. **1869** and **1871.** Cranberry 10-5 thumbprint toy lamps with ball shade and half shade. **1870.** Cranberry toy lamp with swirl motif and ball shade. **1872-1873.** Cranberry toy lamps with swirl motif. **1874.** Cranberry toy lamp with honeycomb motif. **1875-1880.** Moon and Star toy lamps in amber, ruby, milk glass, crystal, amethyst and blue. **1881.** Amethyst toy lamp with swirl motif and opal student shade. **1882.** Amethyst toy lamp with swirl motif, half shade. **1883.** Amethyst toy lamp with opal ball shade. **1884.** Cranberry toy lamp with swirl motif and half shade. **1885-1886.** Blue opalescent toy lamps with swirl and honeycomb motifs (half shades). **1887.** Cabbage Leaf toy lamp in crystal (satin finish). **1888-1892.** Daisy and Cube toy lamps in green, amber, blue, milk glass and amberina.

INDEX

NOTES